Oscar Niemeyer
and
Brazilian Free-form
Modernism

Oscar Niemeyer
and
Brazilian Free-form
Modernism

David Underwood

George Braziller, Inc., New York

For Melissa and Leigh.

First published in 1994 by George Braziller, Inc.
Text copyright © George Braziller, Inc.

Texts and drawings by Oscar Niemeyer and Figures 1a,
36, 45, 69, 79, and 80 copyright © Fundação Oscar
Niemeyer, Rio de Janeiro.

Figures 7, 9-10 copyright © Fondation Le Corbusier.

For information, please address the publisher:
George Braziller, Inc.
60 Madison Avenue
New York, N.Y. 10010

LIBRARY OF CONGRESS CATALOGING-IN PUBLICATION DATA:

Underwood, David Kendrick.
Oscar Niemeyer and Brazilian free-form modernism /
David Underwood.
          p. cm.
Includes bibliographical references.
ISBN 0-8076-1335-5 (cloth). – ISBN 0-8076-1336-3
     (pbk.)
1. Niemeyer, Oscar, 1907- – Criticism and interpretation.
2. International style (Architecture) – Brazil.
3. Architecture, Modern – 20th century – Brazil.
4. Niemeyer, Oscar, 1907-
I. Title.
NA859.N5U5 1994   93-39301
1720'.92—dc20   CIP

Frontispiece illustration: Oscar Niemeyer, Memorial da
América Latina, drawing of bleeding hand sculpture
(see Fig. 92).

Designed by Abby Goldstein
Printed and bound in the United States of America
First edition

CONTENTS

PREFACE AND ACKNOWLEDGMENTS

This book is an exploration of some of the major themes and sources of the work of Oscar Niemeyer, an exploration that seeks to dispel the commonly held misconception, reinforced by much of the critical literature, that Niemeyer's contribution to modern architecture has been essentially a formalistic one. The premise of this study is that meaning is derived from context, and it is precisely the sort of contextual analysis attempted here that has been missing from the art-historical scholarship. An examination of the many and varied contexts in which Niemeyer has worked—physical, historical, cultural, socioeconomic, political, urban, artistic, and theoretical—will do much to clarify the intentions and meaning behind his "formalistic" innovations. Though not all of these contexts can be given full treatment here, this study is offered as a modest step toward a broader thematic appraisal of Niemeyer's achievement within some of them, especially those of Rio de Janeiro and his own and Le Corbusier's theories. I have thus relied heavily on the writings and comments of the architects in seeking to understand the impact of Rio's physical milieu on them.

An analysis comparing Niemeyer's work to the important free-form achievements of postwar Europe and America is also beyond the scope of the present work. What is put forth here is a consideration of the evolution of a distinctly Brazilian free-form mode that celebrates the inherent plasticity of the native curve over the rigid rectilinearity of the International Style. The rise of free-form modernism is generally associated with post–World War II disillusionment with the machine as an aesthetic metaphor and an interest in a more organic architecture. This is most evident in the late styles of such architects as Frank Lloyd Wright, Le Corbusier, and Eero Saarinen. Saarinen's TWA Terminal at New York's John F. Kennedy International Airport (1956–62) and Le Corbusier's

Chapel of Notre Dame du Haut at Ronchamp (1950–54) are good examples of free-form modernism in America and Europe.

Niemeyer's development of free-form modernism actually preceded that of his European and American contemporaries. As early as 1940, in the famous complex of buildings at Pampulha, a suburb of Belo Horizonte, Brazil, he began developing a fluid and lyrical architecture of great sculptural richness. While the point of departure for many of his ideas was the formal and theoretical system of Le Corbusier, who came to Brazil in 1929 and 1936, Niemeyer soon moved away from the rationality of the "five points" to develop the emotive side of Corbusian thought in a way entirely appropriate to the Brazilian setting. His continual dialogue with the natural topographies of Brazil and his creative evolution of the Corbusian discourse into an architecture of the imagination—one with undeniable surrealist qualities—is demonstrated in a number of free-form masterpieces designed between 1940 and the present. These works show that modernism, especially the type born of the interaction between Corbusian theory and tropical reality, can have as much complexity and contradiction, the duality celebrated by Robert Venturi, as any postmodernist could wish for. They also reflect the architect's sensitivity to place and his interest in poetry and transcendental meaning. In Niemeyer's modernism, the creation of architecture is an essentially spiritual act: a response to the monumental permanence of nature that visualizes a poetry of man-made forms based on her design. It is an intensely personal ritual that both liberates the architect and allows him to find integration with the universe.

It is important to emphasize that the term "free-form modernism" does not apply to all of Niemeyer's work—that his fluid style developed slowly, as he learned from his own work and that of his contemporaries. The seminal works of the late 1930s and early 1940s—especially the Brazilian Pavilion for the 1939 New York World's Fair and the Casa do Baile in the Pampulha Complex in Minas Gerais—mark the start of a decade of creative experimentation that culminated in the mature masterpiece of Niemeyer's free-form style: the 1953 Canoas House in Rio de Janeiro. After the first international criticism of his work and a trip to Europe in 1954, Niemeyer moved toward a more disciplined mode of free-form design illustrated by the urbanistic masterpieces of Brasília. Niemeyer's post-Brasília work has been characterized by two broad tendencies. The first is the refinement and expansion of previous ideas and forms in an international context (illustrated by his works in Italy, France, and Algeria in the sixties and seventies); the second is the evolution of the more Surrealistic, free-form style of such ensembles as his late masterpiece, the Memorial da América Latina in São Paulo (1989). Over the course of his long career, Niemeyer's works have maintained a healthy dialogue between disciplined control and freedom of form.

The rise of modernist architecture in Brazil, beginning around 1930 with the advent of Getúlio Vargas, implied neither the immediate achievement of a freedom of form nor a complete negation of the colonial past. Brazil's first modern regime and those since have made it clear that liberty is not for everyone. Politicians and architects alike have embraced and explored certain traditional values in order to arrive at new solutions. In particular, the elitist politics of the old patriarchal system, with its paternalistic authoritarianism, has been reinforced by modern Brazilian regimes and has formed the basis for the patronage of such important Niemeyer works as the Ministry of Education and Health Building in Rio and the recent Memorial da América Latina. Brazilian modernism has involved not only a continuation of colonial power structures and ideologies in new "progressive" forms, but also a rediscovery of colonial Brazilian art and its Baroque values: the prevalence of well-defined hierarchies, the unity of the arts, the concern for scenography and urban monumentality, the search for a universality rooted in specific emotions and local conditions, the faith in all-encompassing dogmas—from the poetic positivism of Le Corbusier and the statist developmentalism of Brasília to the persistent utopianism that characterizes both.

It is perhaps ironic that in attempting to free themselves from the cultural imperialism of the past, especially that of nineteenth-century France, Brazilian architects and patrons turned to yet another foreigner for a reevaluation of their own colonial heritage as a source of forms and meanings. But Le Corbusier was unlike previous "imperialists" in that he was open to a deeper exploration of what the Brazilian milieu—especially the colonial heritage and the physical environment—could contribute to the country's artistic modernization. Such an exploration was also at the heart of Lúcio Costa's and Oscar Niemeyer's search for a Brazilian style. Thus, one of the reasons for the early flowering and subsequent brilliance of Brazilian modernism was the shared interests and sensibility that characterized the collaborative relationship between Le Corbusier and Brazilians like Costa and Niemeyer.

This book has also been a collaborative effort in the best Brazilian sense of the word. My first thanks go to Oscar Niemeyer for opening the doors of his office and foundation to me, and for fitting me into his busy schedule time and again. My work would not have been possible without his permission to research in his archives and reproduce many of the texts and images included herein. Like the architect, I am also indebted to a number of Brazilian men and women who have offered advice, support, and information. Foremost among these is Ana Lúcia Niemeyer de Medeiros, Niemeyer's granddaughter, and the friendly staff of the Fundação Oscar Niemeyer, which she directs. I gained much insight on Niemeyer and Brazilian modernism in general from several interviews with Lúcio Costa, Roberto Burle Marx, and António Carlos Jobim (co-author of the famous "Girl from Ipanema"). My work in Brasília was greatly facilitated by Fernando Andrade, who arranged guided tours of the buildings and offered his expertise and constant good cheer.

My research and travel expenses were funded in part by faculty grants from the Rutgers Research Council and in part by Horsa Hotéis Ltda. of Brazil, which offered me impeccable accommodations in exchange for this all-too-modest acknowledgment of its tremendous contribution to my work. Without the enlightened cultural vision and kindness of Senhor José Augusto T. Boaventura, who for me epitomizes to the utmost the generosity of the Brazilian people, this book would have remained unexecuted.

I would also like to thank Paulo Romeo and Michel Moch for their assistance with the photography for the book. David Brownlee, Nicholas Adams, and Dennis Dollens provided helpful feedback on parts of an earlier draft of the manuscript, and Lisa Vignuolo offered diligent research assistance. I want also to thank George Braziller and my editor at Braziller, Adrienne Baxter, who have been so wonderfully supportive of the project from the start, and my parents, Helen and Joel; my wife, Liliana; my son, Leigh; and finally my daughter, Melissa. Their love and devotion have made all things possible.

D. K. U.
Rio de Janeiro, July 1993

Figures 1a–1b. Oscar Niemeyer in the mid-1950s and in 1992. At eighty-six, Niemeyer has become a Brazilian institution, in the words of Darcy Ribeiro: "the most important cultural event that has ever happened to Brazil."

Figure 1b.

Figure 1a.

I. A CARIOCA ITINERARY

Sprawling in majestic disarray across a strip of land between granite peaks and the south Atlantic, Rio de Janeiro is the final victory of fantasy over fact.

—Edwin Taylor

Oscar Niemeyer Soares Filho (figs. 1a and 1b) is, before anything else, a Carioca, a child of Rio de Janeiro—that marvelous, mountainous city by the sea, a microcosm and magnification of the mystery that is Brazil (fig. 2). It is a place that has stymied the sociologist bent on objective analysis, beguiled the most hardened rationalist, and compelled the most careful planner to abandon his calculations and surrender himself instead to the provocative possibilities of the here and now, the momentary and the fleeting, the breathtaking beauty of the beaches and the bay. It is a place that has inspired great artists—one in particular, the subject of this book—to turn topography into lyrical

Figure 2. View of Ipanema Beach, Rio de Janeiro. Niemeyer's architecture echoes the curving contours of Rio's beaches and hills.

poetry in defiance of all artistic norms and social taboos.

Perhaps more than any other modern architect, Oscar Niemeyer has been the champion of liberty in design—of the unbridled freedom to express oneself against the limitations imposed by history; of the cultural freedom to speak out against the injustices of a persisting colonial reality and the banalities of European academic tradition; of the instinctual freedom to take one's cues from Brazil's topography and to design in accordance with her curves. Niemeyer's architecture is first and foremost a spirited celebration of the tropic and the erotic, of the magical landscapes and sensuous life-style of his native Rio. To study his architecture is thus to embark upon a distinctly Carioca itinerary, a journey that is rooted in the Brazilian place yet transcends it, a journey that reflects the development of the human spirit as it moves from youthful exuberance and rebellion through self-indulgence and self-reflection to the search for an ultimate redemption through art. Some critics have charged that Niemeyer has emphasized dramatic visual effects and the innovation of forms at the expense of functional considerations—an emphasis typical of a city so preoccupied with style and fashionable appearances. A deeper analysis, however, reveals that his art is also profoundly spiritual in its quest for poetic feeling and an intimacy with the infinite. Niemeyer's architecture derives its power from precisely this: while it reflects the multiple dichotomies of the Brazilian experience, it also projects an emotive universality that few architects have been able to achieve.

One of the most basic dichotomies addressed in Niemeyer's life and work is the confrontation between the shackles of the colonial past and the culture of Catholicism, on the one hand, and the personal and social freedom of an imagined future, on the other. The world into which Niemeyer was born on December 15, 1907, was anchored firmly in the patriarchal family values of colonial tradition, in which sexual roles, social mores, and other cultural givens were clearly defined by the conventional binary categories of premodern society: master and servant, male and female, aristocrat and commoner, aesthete and craftsman. Niemeyer reminisces about his family's old colonial-style home in Laranjeiras, a picturesque hillside neighborhood of cobblestoned streets and nineteenth-century mansions, and the most sought after residential area among the governing elite of the old Brazilian capital. His fondest childhood memories are of the house at number 26 Rua Manoel, a steeply sloped street that today bears the name of his grandfather Ribeiro de Almeida, in his day a distinguished minister in the Federal Supreme Court. Niemeyer's upbringing was one of privilege and comfort, but his nostalgia is compromised by his dissatisfaction with the social injustices of the world into which he was born, a world in which, he once observed, "corruption seemed to play an integral part."[1] For all its playfulness and sensual exuberance, Niemeyer's architecture reverberates with a utopian social idealism that makes it far more than a personal sentimental journey. A rebel in spirit, he has dreamed of freedom not just for the artist but for the exploited masses as well.

While the patriarchal society of colonial Brazil and an intimate friendship with his father were the anchors of his childhood security, nature and a nurturing relationship with Brazilian women became the key to his sense of personal and cultural freedom and to an artistic future hardly imaginable. The affection and attention Oscar received from his mother, Delfina Almeida de Niemeyer Soares, who died when he was twenty-one, and from his cousin "Milota" (Emilia Adelaide de Almeida e Albuquerque) led him to observe later on that he had two mothers. In fact, he had three.

Figure 3. View of Sugar Loaf
Mountain, Botafogo, and Guanabara
Bay. Rio de Janeiro is a symphony
of natural and man-made
architectures.

The colonial-style veranda that stretched around
the front of the family home commanded a magnificent view of Guanabara Bay. The gentle curves of
Sugar Loaf Mountain (fig. 3) visually nurtured the
child whose first and most important teacher was
the incredibly fecund Mother Nature of the tropics,
a fertility goddess who would enchant and entice
him throughout his adult life. Ever visible in the
distance from his studio window overlooking
Copacabana Beach, she continues to beckon to him
today, like some fateful siren of ancient maritime
lore.

   Like a child growing into awkward adolescence,
the Brazilian society of Niemeyer's youth was in
transition. The Industrial Revolution, a latecomer to
a world ruled by oligarchic coffee barons, chal-
lenged the old order with new urban problems, a
new immigrant population, and new progressive
ideas. But industrialization did not free Brazil from
its colonial past. Rio in the early twentieth century

was a city marked by its commercial and cultural dependency on Europe: a society dominated by its infatuation with French fashion, by its lust for British capital, and by the inferiority complex of the Brazilian elite, who continued to prefer London and Paris to their own cities. Well into the century, Brazilian artists still imitated European styles in an attempt to forge a new modern order that would erase from their collective memory the perceived barbarities of their embarrassing colonial heritage.

In urban design and architecture, the symbols of this ideology of Europeanization, or "civilization," as it was officially known, were the Avenida Central and the Teatro Municipal (fig. 4), begun respectively in the first decade of this century by the French-trained engineer Francisco de Pereira Passos (mayor of Rio from 1902 to 1906) and his grandson, who drew their inspiration from the boulevards and

Figure 4. Oliveira Passos et al., Teatro Municipal, Rio de Janeiro, 1905–9, main façade. Modeled after Garnier's Paris Opera House, the Municipal Theater symbolized the Carioca elite's preference for French haute culture and the urban tastes of Paris.

Opera House of Paris. It was the Teatro Municipal's aura of upper-middle-class respectability, Beaux-Arts conformity, and European hegemony that the architecture of Niemeyer would come to challenge and overturn. What he wanted above all else was an architecture that would be true to Brazil, to Rio, and to his own rebellious conscience. At the heart of Niemeyer's best work is a series of conscious revolts—first against European academic-historical architecture, then against the rectilinear geometries of the International Style and the orthodox structural rationalities that stood in the way of the creation of what he called "a space for the imagination."

But there was little in Niemeyer's boyhood to foreshadow this spirit of protest or the talents that would blossom spontaneously in the 1940s. He confesses that his main concern until he was fifteen was soccer.[2] More than just a childhood game, soccer for Niemeyer and the Brazilians is a national passion, something taken as seriously as carnival or the design of a good building. Soccer, like the competitions of the samba schools during carnival, reveals a dynamic expression of free gestures and curving, independent motions. Beyond the landscape of Rio and the swaying bodies of the *sambistas*, only the dynamic arcing trajectory of the soccer ball—a pure solid moving freely in space—provides an anticipation of the fluid curvilinear lines we find later in Niemeyer's freely improvised sketches. Perhaps as important, soccer, like carnival and the making of a new architecture, is a ritual event in which the common man can find some sort of escape from reality, perhaps become a hero, and express a larger national aspiration. Such reveries were in the realm of Niemeyer's first drawing exercises, which were so spontaneous as to be free of the need for paper and pencil. Instead, in Niemeyer's personal design ritual, the air is his medium, his finger a pen. His recollection of his first works of art focuses on drawings made in space with his finger: light, airy, ethereal, floating—forms born of the flights of a youthful imagination. As he recalls, "I was drawing forms that I kept in my memory, that I corrected and developed as if I had really designed them."[3] Seventy years later, he still fantasizes (and designs) in this way.

The compelling connection between the airborne fantasies of Niemeyer's adolescence and his mature work as a designer resides in his confession that he decided to become an architect because he liked to draw. Prior to 1930, the year he entered Rio's fine arts academy, the Escola Nacional de Belas Artes, an architectural profession as such hardly existed in Brazil: building tradesmen and civil engineers dominated the design and especially the construction process. The conflict between the technical priorities of the engineer and the creative goals of the artist was reinforced by the split in architectural education between the scientific emphasis of the polytechnical schools of Rio and São Paulo and the fine arts emphasis of the academy. The first faculty to issue a diploma for the practice of architecture (in a course separate from the fine arts academy) was created in Rio in 1936, the year of Le Corbusier's proposed reorganization of the national university system.

Niemeyer's early approach to architecture as primarily a matter of drawing is clearly rooted in the academy's definition of architecture as a fine art that is conceived independently of technical and social considerations. His continuing dependence on structural engineers (*calculistas*) and his refusal to be shackled by social preoccupations are, at least in part, legacies of the old academy. But because of the incomplete and anachronistic training it provided, the evolution of Niemeyer's thinking depended considerably on the examples set by pioneering individuals who dared to go beyond the narrow confines of institutional instruction—Lúcio Costa and Le Corbusier, in particular.

Niemeyer came under the influence of Costa first, the spiritual father of Brazilian modernism and a champion of Le Corbusier's "sacred book of architecture" (*Vers une architecture*). Born in Toulon, France, Costa received his early education in England and Switzerland and his artistic training in Rio's academy, where he studied from 1917 to 1922. A modest man of immense culture and erudition, Costa was as sensitive to Brazilian traditions as he was attuned to the latest avant-garde ideas of Europe. His appreciation of European modernism was stimulated by travel to the Continent in the late 1920s and by his analysis of the works of Perret and Le Corbusier. It was Costa who, in the context of the political upheaval of 1930 and the rise of the bureaucratic-authoritarian regime of Getúlio Vargas, began the reform of the outmoded Beaux-Arts curriculum of the academy and thus prepared the way for the modernist revolution in Brazilian design. To supplement the course offerings of the older professors, Costa contracted a group of young instructors from outside the academy, all of whom were committed to European avant-garde ideals. Among them were the German functionalist Alexander Buddeus, who promoted the ideas of Walter Gropius, and Gregori Warchavchik, a Russian émigré whose own residence in São Paulo (1927–28) was the first modernist house erected in Brazil. Costa's appointments, introduced at the very start of Niemeyer's architectural education, gave young Brazilian architects a clear choice between the old and the new. But Costa's sensitivity to history and his appreciation of certain classical values in architecture led him to insist on a modern architecture that did not turn its back on the past.

It was under Costa's protective wing that Niemeyer's talents as a draftsman and architect were nurtured. After graduating from the academy in 1934, Niemeyer went to work as a volunteer in the office of Costa, who provided him with ample opportunity to develop his art. On more than one occasion, Costa generously stepped aside to let the younger man reveal his talent. The first time came in 1936, when he allowed his inexperienced draftsman to join the definitive team of Brazilian architects collaborating with Le Corbusier on the Ministry of Education and Health Building in Rio. Then in 1938, after winning the competition for the design of the Brazilian Pavilion for the 1939 New York World's Fair, Costa set aside his own project and invited Niemeyer to collaborate with him on a new one. In 1940 he again encouraged his protégé to take on a project that he, with his superior knowledge of Brazil's colonial architecture, would normally have tackled: the Grand Hotel in Ouro Preto, the old colonial capital of the mining state of Minas Gerais.

Costa also fostered in Niemeyer an appreciation of the Lusitanian architecture brought by the Portuguese colonizers and adapted to the Brazilian environment in the seventeenth and eighteenth centuries. For Costa, Brazil's colonial architecture contained the seeds of truth for the modern style he envisioned: its constructional honesty, volumetric unity, and formal integrity—not to mention its appropriateness to the tropical environment and its sculptural qualities—led him to promote its preservation through the Serviço do Patrimônio Histórico e Artístico Nacional, and to explore its qualities in his own designs.[4] Costa's sober reevaluation of the colonial as a source for Brazilian modernist design was crucial for moving Brazilian architects away from the fashionable façades of historical and neocolonial styles. Following Costa's lead, Niemeyer created a richly sculptural and scenographic architecture that reflected what Leopoldo Castedo has called the "Baroque prevalence in Brazilian art."[5]

While appreciative of the Baroque plasticity and cultural setting of Brazil's colonial buildings—his favorite, the early-eighteenth-century church of N. S. da Glória do Outeiro in Rio (figs. 5 and 6), is an

Figure 5. J. Cardoso Ramalho, Church of Nossa Senhora da Glória do Outeiro, Rio de Janeiro, ca. 1740. An execellent example of the colonial Baroque architecture left by the Portuguese, the Glória is admired by Costa and Niemeyer for its sculptural and scenographic qualities.

exquisite example—Niemeyer soon turned to more vital sources for inspiration. Like Le Corbusier, who was deeply moved by the seductive curves and imposing sculptural presence of Rio's tropical landscape, Niemeyer possesses a sensibility too open to the here and now, the free and sensual, to be submerged in theoretical speculation or anchored to a colonial past (especially one so heavily laden with painful associations with imperial exploitation, a past still too strongly remembered by his generation). What he sought instead was a new cultural statement, a free-form architectural expression made possible by the technical potentials of reinforced concrete, a freedom rooted in the rich and diverse landscapes of Brazil, especially the curving contours of the mountains, beaches, and bays of his beloved *cidade maravilhosa* (marvelous city). As Le Corbusier once told him: "Oscar, you always have the mountains of Rio in your eyes. You do Baroque in reinforced concrete, but you do it very well."[6]

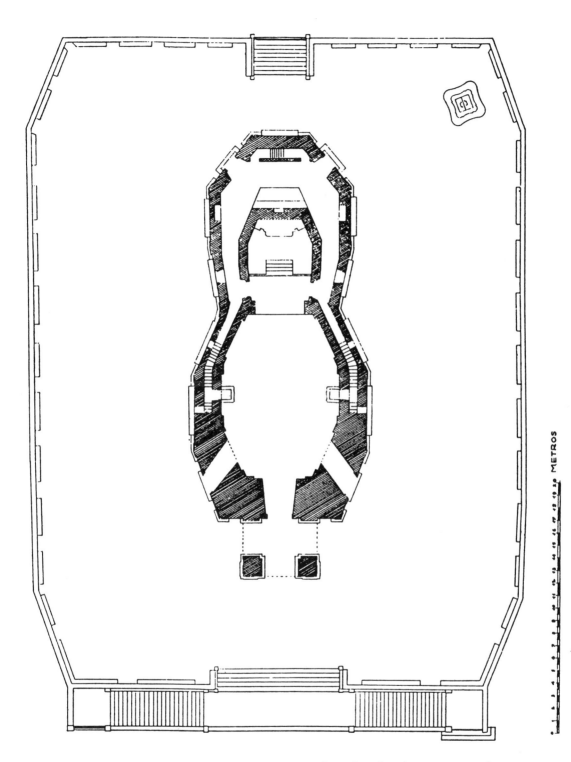

Figure 6. N. S. da Glória do Outeiro, plan. The design reflects the colonial interest in curvilinear form and interlocking volumes that typified the Baroque and Niemeyer's modernism.

Rio de Janeiro and the Discourse of Le Corbusier

Niemeyer's achievement of a richly sculptural, free-form modernism that explored the composition and poetic implications of his tropical ambience grew from his attentiveness to the formal and theoretical discourses of Le Corbusier. The single most important factor in Niemeyer's artistic evolution, aside from his Carioca upbringing and the mentoring of Lúcio Costa, was the influence of the Franco-Swiss master and especially the opportunity to work with him in 1936, when Gustavo Capenema, Minister of Education and Health under President Vargas, invited Le Corbusier to come to Rio as a design consultant and offer a series of seminars on modern architecture. Le Corbusier had been to Rio once before, in 1929, and had left an inspired plan for the city's re-urbanization (fig. 7). The design responded to the curving contours in a deliberately dramatic, horizontal sweep that answered to the capricious verticality of the mountains. It was a poetic response of unprecedented boldness and spontaneity, and it charged the Brazilians' imagination.[7]

Like Rio's topography, Brazilian culture is a vibrant celebration of the curved and the curving. Whereas European rationalism has generally sought the closest distance between two points—the straight line—Brazil and Niemeyer have taken a more scenic route. It could be argued that it was in Latin America that modern architecture in the West lost its rationalist purity and puritanical morality to the natural forces of the native curve. While Frank Lloyd Wright preached his fire-and-brimstone sermons from the rectilinear pews of Unity Temple and the upright dining chairs of the Prairie house, Le Corbusier underwent a fundamental shift in artistic sensibility in response to his experience of South America. Espying the grandeur of nature and the curving contours of the Paraguay and Paraná rivers from the window of an airship, he saw the creative possibilities of the waters' meandering lines in an instantaneous realization in which "everything took on the precision of a tracing."[8] The

Figure 7. Le Corbusier, Plan for Rio de Janeiro, 1929. Le Corbusier responded poetically to the verticality of Rio's mountains with a utopian composition of insistent horizontals. Rio's housing problem was to be solved by a continuous apartment block elevated on pilotis and surmounted by a superhighway that connected Rio's neighborhoods.

music that fused Latin, Indian, and African influences, he reflected, was similarly curved and lyrical. So overwhelmed was he with the power and inevitability of the meander that he made it first an "affecting theorem," then a law and metaphor, an organizing principle for the creative process of the gifted artist: "a phenomenon of cyclical development absolutely similar to creative thinking, to human invention. . . . Following the outlines of the meander from above," he said, "I understood the difficulties met in human affairs, the dead ends in which they get stuck and the apparently miraculous

solutions that suddenly resolve apparently inextricable situations."[9] Le Corbusier extrapolated the artistic and social lessons of the Law of the Meander in these terms:

I draw a river. The goal is precise: to get from one point to another: river or idea. A slight incident takes place, the incidents of the spirit: immediately, a small slight bend, hardly noticeable. The water is thrown to the left, it digs into the bank; from there, by reaction, it is thrown back to the right. Then the straight line disappears. To the left, to the right, always deeper, the water bites, hollows, cuts away; always wider, the idea seeks its way. The straight line has become sinuous; the idea has acquired incidents. The sinuousness becomes characteristic, the meander appears; the idea is ramified. Soon the solution has become frightfully complicated, it is a paradox. . . . The objective is respected: one moves toward the goal, but on what a path![10]

As this passage makes clear, Le Corbusier saw the meander as a metaphor for a process of conceptual clarification in which "a pure idea has burst forth, a solution has appeared." Its lessons led him to conclude: "Moments of 'simplicity' are the unknotting of acute and critical crises of complication."[11]

As a metaphor for the creative process and social problem solving, the Law of the Meander aptly anticipates the Brazilian free-form approach that came to characterize the work of Niemeyer. In social and artistic terms, the Brazilian counterpart to the Law of the Meander is the *jeito*, an irrepressible method that deals with obstacles by going around them. The *jeito* pronounces the power of individual creativity over rigid rules and systems. For a fortunate few like Niemeyer, this cult of individual creativity has become a social institution.

But the *jeito* is more than the characteristically Brazilian ability always to find a way out by finding a way around. It describes the Brazilian style—the lightness of touch, the graceful elegance of form and movement inherent in the sauntering "Girl from Ipanema" and celebrated in the best of

Brazilian modernism. Niemeyer's architecture reflects the meandering Brazilian *jeito* in both its sinuous, sensual style and its improvisational, extemporaneous way of coping with life.

Costa commented that prior to Niemeyer's contact with Le Corbusier in 1936, the young architect had worked industriously in his office but "without showing the least sign of talent."[12] But the impact of Le Corbusier on Niemeyer's artistic spirit was magical and immediate, and went far beyond the younger man's assimilation of Le Corbusier's prescribed "five points of a new architecture" (pilotis, free plan, free façade, ribbon windows, and roof garden). What impressed Niemeyer most were the spontaneity of Le Corbusier's sketching method and the freedom of his conceptualization. Le Corbusier's improvisations reinforced the tendency toward design fluidity that was instinctive but as yet undeveloped in the youthful Niemeyer. For the first time in the history of Brazilian architecture, a European architect was imposing on his colonial followers a spirited system that would have the effect of setting at least some of them free.

The liberating impact of the Corbusian discourse was not immediately evident in architecture, however, for the patronage of the authoritarian Vargas regime was more interested in social control than artistic freedom. The advent of Vargas in 1930 hastened the transformation of the Brazil of coffee barons and rural workers into an urban Brazil of busy boulevards (fig. 8) and wretched slums. Vargas envisioned a state run by an efficient bureaucracy of technocrats and enterpreneurs who would fuel the prosperity of the nation and promote new cultural symbols and a positivistic view of the future. As a young man in his late twenties, Niemeyer played an important role in this transformation through his involvement in the design of the first major monument of the modern movement in South America: the Ministry of Education and Health Building in Rio (1936–43). The building

(figs. 9–12) was the complex product of a six-week collaboration between Le Corbusier and a group of Brazilian architects headed by Costa, among whom Niemeyer would soon emerge as the most important. It was in the context of the collaborative design that Niemeyer observed and absorbed the style of Le Corbusier.

The Ministry project reflected the dilemma of Brazil's dependent artistic development: in seeking a symbol of national modernization, the Brazilians embraced Corbusian forms and a European ideology. Corbusian theories and methods were readily accepted because they were seen as appropriate to the climate of Brazil's new political regime and to the technical possibilities of an industrializing nation where reinforced concrete was much more accessible than steel. But Le Corbusier was not just another European promoting a purely rational architecture or the imitation of Continental metropolitan styles: he was hopelessly seduced by Brazil—especially its exuberant topography and solar radiance—and by the Brazilians themselves—particularly their sporting life-style and poetic sensibility ("how their hearts are wide open to things of the spirit"[13]). Le Corbusier was forever changed by the interaction—and so was Niemeyer, who quickly absorbed the more important lessons of the Franco-Swiss master, then turned them to new expressive purposes. For the Ministry building, he worked out a number of studied refinements to the "five points" that relieved the Corbusian slab with a touch of *jeito*: he elevated the height of the pilotis and made the sun breakers movable, thereby giving the building the freer, lighter, more dynamic quality that would become the hallmark of his later work. As Costa summarized the significance of the Corbusian episode in Rio: "Never had architecture gone through such a rapid change in so short a time."[14]

The first stage of Niemeyer's artistic rebellion was thus completely in line with Le Corbusier's

Figure 8 (opposite). Avenida Presidente Vargas, Rio de Janeiro, begun 1940. One of the symbols of the modernizing regime of Getúlio Vargas, the avenue was cast as one of the widest boulevards in the world, powerful testimony to the Brazilian commitment to progress. Hundreds of colonial buildings, including churches and tenement houses, were destroyed to make way for it.

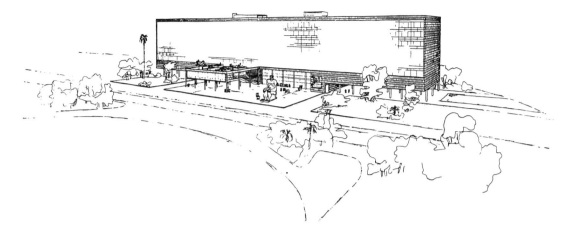

Figure 9. Le Corbusier, first project for the Ministry of Education and Health Building, Rio de Janeiro, 1936. Le Corbusier's project for the waterfront site on the Praia Santa Luzia called for a horizontal slab on pilotis.

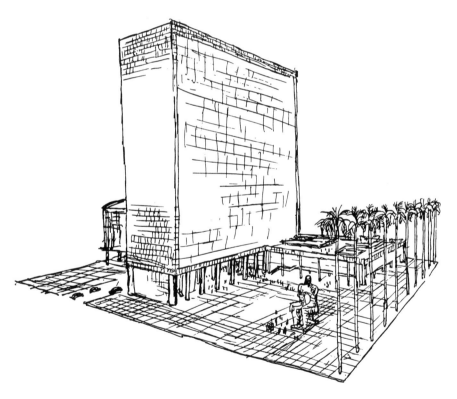

Figure 10. Le Corbusier, sketch showing the definitive development of the Ministry of Education and Health Building. Taking as their point of departure Le Corbusier's second project for a center-city site, the Brazilian team (Lúcio Costa, Oscar Niemeyer, Carlos Leão, Affonso Reidy, Jorge Moreira, and Ernani Vasconcelos) modified the project to create a more vertical composition with adjustable sun breakers. The changes resulted in a more monumental, structurally lighter, and plastically richer work that was thoroughly Brazilian.

Figures 11–12. Lúcio Costa, Oscar Niemeyer,
Le Corbusier, et al., Ministry of Education
and Health Building, Rio de Janeiro,
1936–43, plans. The layout of the ministry
reflected the integration of multiple functions
into a simple, unified T-plan.

Figure 11 a–b.

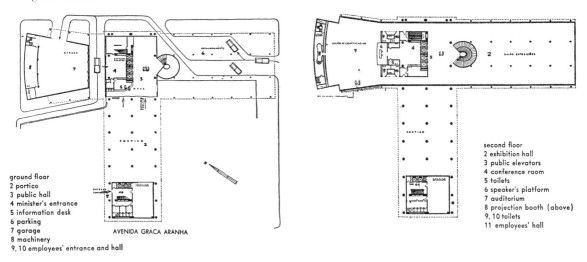

ground floor
2 portico
3 public hall
4 minister's entrance
5 information desk
6 parking
7 garage
8 machinery
9, 10 employees' entrance and hall

second floor
2 exhibition hall
3 public elevators
4 conference room
5 toilets
6 speaker's platform
7 auditorium
8 projection booth (above)
9, 10 toilets
11 employees' hall

Figure 12 a–b.

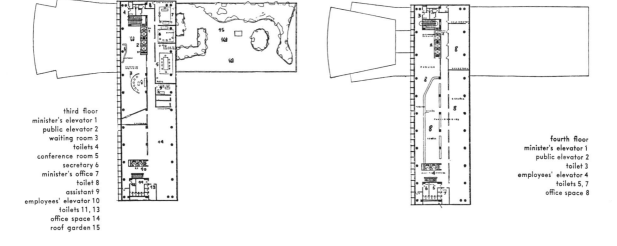

third floor
minister's elevator 1
public elevator 2
waiting room 3
toilets 4
conference room 5
secretary 6
minister's office 7
toilet 8
assistant 9
employees' elevator 10
toilets 11, 13
office space 14
roof garden 15

fourth floor
minister's elevator 1
public elevator 2
toilet 3
employees' elevator 4
toilets 5, 7
office space 8

attack on academic traditions and his call for an architecture of poetic emotion. Both of these had been forcefully expressed in Le Corbusier's two major early writings, *Vers une architecture* (1923) and especially *Précisions* (1930). In the first lecture in the latter book, he wrote of the need "to free oneself entirely" of the "suffocating constraint" of academic thinking, and demanded that modern architects "denounce academicism in the name of all that is deepest in our hearts" and replace it with poetry. Whereas the academician is "one who accepts results without verifying their causes . . . and does not involve his own self in every question," the poet "is the visionary, the reader of the event . . . who shows a new truth."[15]

Rio de Janeiro offered the visionary a dazzling event of nature that openly revealed its truths without having to be analyzed. For Le Corbusier, "the whole site began to speak, on the water, on earth, in the air; it spoke of architecture" in "a poem of human geometry and immense natural fantasy."[16] His definition of architecture as "the masterly, correct, and magnificent play of masses brought together in light" took on new relevance and visual intensity in the dramatic topography of sun-drenched Rio. There, the "great primary forms which light reveals to advantage" were visible everywhere: in the mountains, in the people, in the colonial architecture of pure white volumetric shapes left by the Portuguese. In its undulating rivers and white crescent beaches, the city offered a delightful diversity of radiant profiles and contours—"the touchstones of the architect," as Le Corbusier called them. Rio's perspectives were naturally conducive to the Corbusian concept of architecture as a "plastic thing, something seen and measured by the eyes," as well as to the fundamental goal of the architect "to establish emotional relationships by means of raw materials."[17]

Le Corbusier described in moving lyrical images how Brazil's tropical summer and Rio's "unforgetable magic" fired him with enthusiasm: the city was "red and pink from its soil, green with its vegetation, blue from the sea; waves break with a little foam on numerous beaches; everything rises; islands piercing the water, peaks falling into it, high hills and great mountains; its wharves are the most beautiful in the world; the sand of the ocean comes to the edge of the houses and palaces; an immense light puts its motor in your heart."[18] It was a place that seduced the artist out of his academic cage, especially "when everything is a festival, when, after two and a half months of constraint and inhibition, everything breaks out in a festival . . . everything is festival and spectacle, all is joy in you, everything contracts itself to retain the newborn idea, everything leads to the joy of creation."[19]

Free-form Modernism and the Architecture of the Brazilian Woman

The Corbusian denunciation of academic thinking transcended purely artistic concerns and was accompanied by a defiance of social taboos: "The biblical dogma that begins by defining as sin the fundamental law of nature, the act of making love, has rotted our hearts."[20] Implied in Le Corbusier's unstated alternative to this repressive dogma is the suggestion that sexual as well as artistic freedom are central values of the modern artist. As he put it, "It is the concept of life that must change; it is the concept of happiness that must be made clear."[21] The fulfillment of basic human impulses must be the starting point, because "the emotions that architecture arouses spring from physical conditions which are inevitable, irrefutable, and today forgotten."[22] Niemeyer went even further: "Architecture is my permanent 'hobby,' but I think that man was born to reproduce like the other animals on earth. And that's why woman is his principal objective. She is part of my life and my architecture."[23] In Rio, where both men relished the view of the beautiful women of Copacabana, the joy of artistic creation is often articulated in sexual terms that equate woman with nature. As Le Corbusier expressed his feelings and method in Rio, "A violent desire comes to you, crazy perhaps, to try a human enterprise here too, the desire to play a match for two, a match of the 'affirmation of mankind' against or with the 'presence of nature.'"[24] The Corbusian discourse proposed a series of antagonistic dualities that suggested the European (male) conquest over the colonial (female).

Niemeyer's free-form modernism involves a similar affirmation of a basically sexual duality. In appropriating the natural forms of women, however, he reveals his mastery of the power of artistic seduction as the most effective means of conquest. While grounded in the Corbusian discourse, Niemeyer found in the natural architectures of Brazil a source of new, more expressive forms that fulfilled his quest for organic unity and an instinctual harmony between man's creative impulses and his natural environment. The strength of his best work is that, while it partakes of the Corbusian theory, it returns directly to Brazilian landscapes and human forms for inspiration.

As Niemeyer matured as an architect, he rejected the rational side of Le Corbusier in favor of the poetic, emotive side, which was closer to his own sensibility and to that of Brazil. He explains how his free-form architecture arose as a protest against what he calls "rational architecture"—the rectilinear, mechanized forms of the International Style: "Everything started when I began the Pampulha studies—my first phase—deliberately despising the exalted right angle and the rationalist architecture made by ruler and square. . . . I protested against this monotonous and repetitive architecture, so easy to elaborate that in a short time it spread quickly from the United States to Japan."[25] Speaking of the sources of the varied curves and the unexpected boldness of his first free-form works, the architect writes: "The intended protest arose from the environment where I lived, with its white beaches, its huge mountains, its old Baroque churches, and its beautiful tanned women. I had within me not only Rio's mountains, as Le Corbusier once observed, but everything that touched me emotionally."[26] These four elements—white beaches, huge mountains, old Baroque churches, and beautiful tanned women—formed the stuff of Niemeyer's dreams and best creations. Common to all is the sensual and free-flowing curve: the tropical *jeito* of Brazil and the basis of his aesthetic.

Even more than Le Corbusier's, Niemeyer's artistic philosophy expounds the virtues of nature over those of engineering and the machine, his own attention to the "lessons of Rio" over Le Corbusier's "lessons of Rome." While Le Corbusier was clearly moved by Rio, his quintessential attitude was that of the theorist who criticized modern architects for having "eyes which do not see," for being blind to the new models of the modern style: the ocean liner, with its clean lines, functional volumes, and sleek proportions; the airplane, which addressed a problem and clearly solved it; and the automobile, which reflected the perfection of a standard type. By 1940, however, these very models for the new rational architecture of Europe had become the source of Niemeyer's Brazilian revolt. Niemeyer offered the world three new reminders: first, Rio's topography of mountains and beaches; second, the colonial churches of the Brazilian past; and third, representing the eternal but ever-changing human present, the suntanned sea nymph of Copacabana (figs. 13 and 14). These were all things that the eyes of the modern Brazilian architect could not avoid seeing. These were the elements that "meandered" the architect with "incidents of the spirit."

While the Corbusian lesson of the airplane lay in the logic of a problem recognized and rationally solved, Niemeyer's lesson of the Brazilian woman lies in the unending mystery and magic that she holds for the poetic spirit inescapably drawn to her. Niemeyer's most significant (and most human) rebellion against European modernist architecture was thus his replacement of International Style functionalism with a new implicit recipe: "form follows [female] beauty." As he put it, "When a form creates beauty, it becomes functional and thus fundamental in architecture."

Figure 13 (opposite, above). Niemeyer, drawing of a Brazilian woman, ink and watercolor. Niemeyer's women are one with Rio's natural elements: sand, surf, and sky.

Figure 14 (opposite, below). Niemeyer, drawing of a Brazilian woman, ink and watercolor. According to Niemeyer's "Poem of the Curve," which accompanies this drawing, female form is an important source of his architecture.

II. THE NATURAL, THE SURREAL, AND THE BEAUTIFUL

Architecture is the first manifestation of man creating his own universe, creating it in the image of nature, submitting to the laws of nature, the laws which govern our own nature, our universe.

—Le Corbusier

Niemeyer found more in the landscapes of his Brazilian universe than spiritual inspiration and a meandering alternative to the hard-edge forms created by Europeans. His most effective architecture reflects his sensitivity to both the poetic possibilities and practical limitations of particular sites. While never determining his lyrical or rebellious intentions, an analysis of a building's proposed site and immediate surroundings is generally the point of departure for his compositions and their synthesis of the natural, the surreal, and the beautiful. Niemeyer's interest in the poetics of the place transcends architecture to incorporate such basic natural elements as sky and clouds, sea and soil, jungle, and hill. Moralizing critics have complained of the excessively formalistic quality of Niemeyer's work, thus demonstrating above all that they have misunderstood his objectives and the cultural tendencies of Brazil—or, more accurately, that they disagreed with them.[27] For Niemeyer, architecture is always about something much bigger than the forms themselves, something much more than what the eye sees in an optical sense. It is a search for permanence and belonging in a changing and sometimes hostile universe, an attempt to find harmony where chaos often reigns, a multimedia experience that engages the human senses and spirit in an episode of imaginative freedom and fantasy.

Niemeyer's most characteristic search has been for an architecture that celebrates curved and sensual form in a feat of structural magic that conjures up an equally magical space. In his most successful architecture, he achieves these attributes, thus demonstrating that his concept of beauty, and thus of spirituality, is rooted as much in the surreal as in the natural. Indeed, Niemeyer's supreme achievement has been his synthesis, or neutralization, of opposing attributes and the aesthetic resolution of the paradox. His best works prior to the early 1950s explored the formal and structural implications of his rebellion against the straight line, but by the mid 1950s and the work in Brasília, these explorations had expanded into the broader realm of a surreal space for the imagination. It is typical of Niemeyer's personal poetry that his deepest fantasies seem always to stem from human forms.

In the first mature Brazilian adaptation of the International Style, the Brazilian Pavilion at the 1939 New York World's Fair (figs. 15–18), Lúcio Costa and Niemeyer collaborated in a spirited exploration of the Corbusian architectural promenade for an exhibition structure that was to showcase the tropical exoticism of their homeland. The pavilion's qualities of fluidity, flexibility, and grace were a product of the architects' efforts to adapt their building to a curving corner site adjacent to that of the imposing French Pavilion. The centerpiece was a lily pond and tropical garden. Costa and Niemeyer created a curving, free-flowing space that successfully integrated exterior and interior through a keen awareness of the "roving-eye" syndrome, a phenomenon familiar enough to the beach-worshiping Carioca but perhaps best described by Le

Figure 15. Costa and Niemeyer, Brazilian Pavilion for the New York World's Fair, 1939. The interior displays were designed by Paul Lester Wiener. According to Costa, who invited Niemeyer to collaborate on the project, the pavilion launched Niemeyer's career internationally.

Figure 16. Brazilian Pavilion, view of lily pond and glazed façade. The centerpiece of the design, visible from all angles as one walked through the pavilion, was the lily pond and tropical garden. The architects sought to evoke the natural milieu of tropical Rio as a means of defining a Brazilian architectural identity. (Stamo Papadaki, *Oscar Niemeyer* [New York: Braziller, 1960], fig. 58; courtesy F. S. Lincoln.)

Figure 17. Brazilian Pavilion, main façade. The design exploited the Corbusian *promenade architecturale*, *jeu de rampes*, and *marriage de contour* in a spirited showcase of Brazilian culture. (Papadaki, *Niemeyer*, fig. 57; courtesy F. S. Lincoln.)

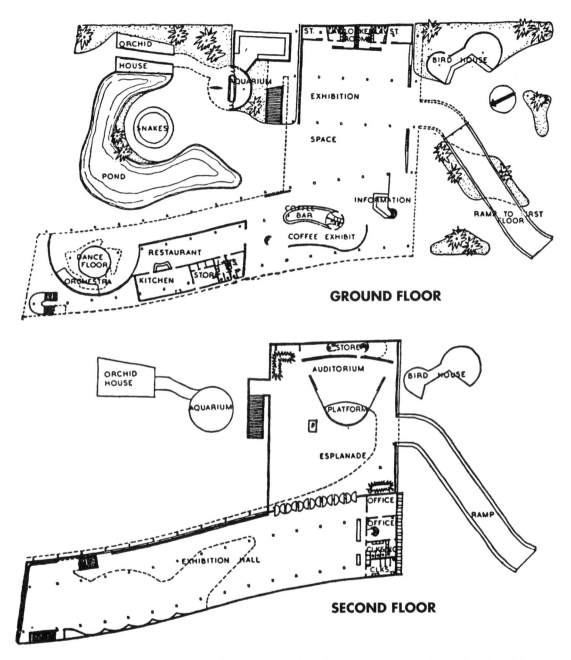

Figure 18. Brazilian Pavilion, plans. The layout, based on the subtle contrasts of curved and straight lines, reflects the architects' desire to create a fluid composition defined by a heightened sense of spatial continuity.

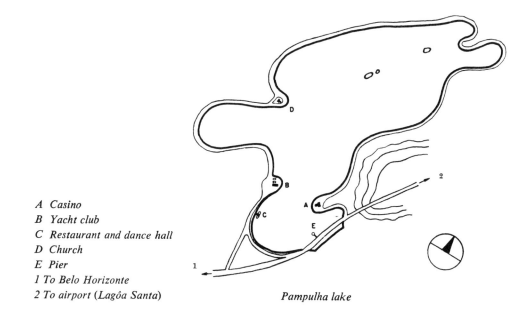

A Casino
B Yacht club
C Restaurant and dance hall
D Church
E Pier
1 To Belo Horizonte
2 To airport (Lagôa Santa)

Pampulha lake

Figure 19. Pampulha, suburb of Belo Horizonte, plan of lake showing location of Niemeyer's buildings, 1940–43. The monuments were unified only by their common commitment to formal innovation and by their scenographic siting along the lake.

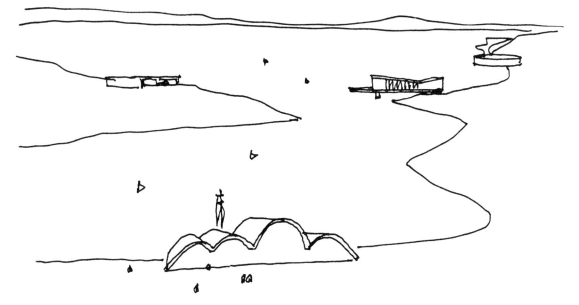

Figure 20. Niemeyer, sketch of monuments on lake at Pampulha, 1940. The Pampulha buildings were conceived not as parts of an ensemble but as symbols of individual freedom—Niemeyer's first "carnival of forms."

Corbusier: "The human eye, in its investigations, is always on the move and the beholder himself is always turning right and left, and shifting about. He is interested in everything and is attracted towards the center of gravity of the whole site. At once the problem spreads to the surroundings."[28]

Niemeyer of course was much more comfortable in Brazilian surroundings than in New York. His first independent statement of free-form modernism came in 1940, when he was commissioned by Juscelino Kubitschek, the mayor of Belo Horizonte and future president of the republic, to design a suburban playground for the newly rich of the industrializing capital of the state of Minas Gerais. Niemeyer's work in the suburb of Pampulha was meant as a carnival of forms for a freewheeling elite, a leisure complex complete with a casino (figs. 21–24), yacht club (figs. 25 and 26), dance hall and restaurant (figs. 27–29), a weekend house for the mayor, a small chapel dedicated to St. Francis (figs. 32–35), and even a hotel (figs. 30 and 31), which was, however, not executed.

Figure 21. Niemeyer, Casino at Pampulha, 1942, main façade. Structural engineer: Joaquim Cardoso. The Casino was to be the focal point of the freewheeling nightlife of Pampulha. Niemeyer's suburban playground for the elite of Belo Horizonte was commissioned by the city's mayor, Juscelino Kubitschek.

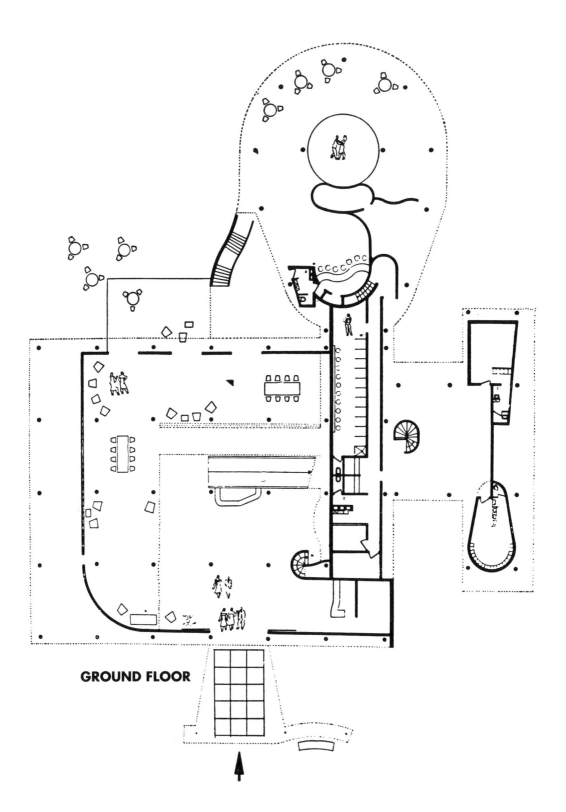

GROUND FLOOR

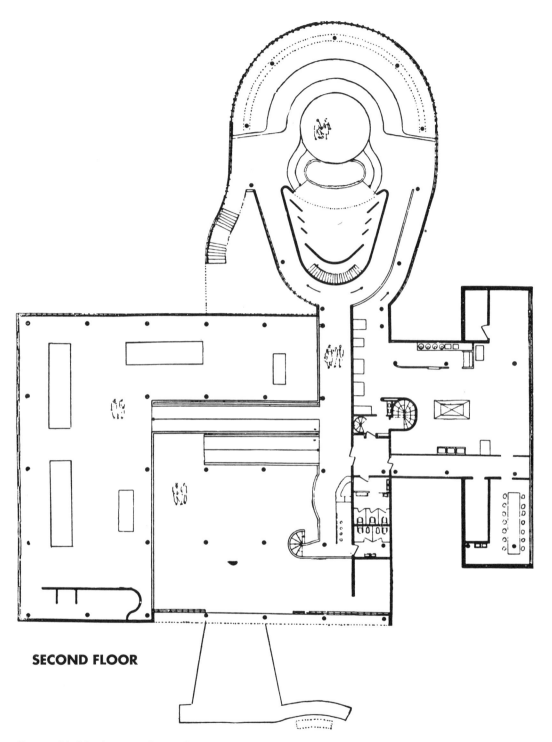

SECOND FLOOR

Figures 22–23. Casino at Pampulha, plans. Niemeyer's *promenade architecturale* was based on the visitor's dynamic experience of ramps, multiple levels, and connecting corridors. Shortly after the building's opening, gambling was outlawed in Brazil. Today it functions as an art musuem.

Figure 24. Casino at Pampulha, main façade at night. The casino's design relied on formal contrasts such as light and dark and on the complex interplay of spaces and volumes for the creation of a magical visual effect. (Courtesy Marcel Gautherot).

Figure 25. Niemeyer, Yacht Club at Pampulha, 1942, sketch of main façade.
Structural engineer: Joaquim Cardoso. The inverted roof recalls that of Le Corbusier's 1930 project for the Erazuriz House in Chile.

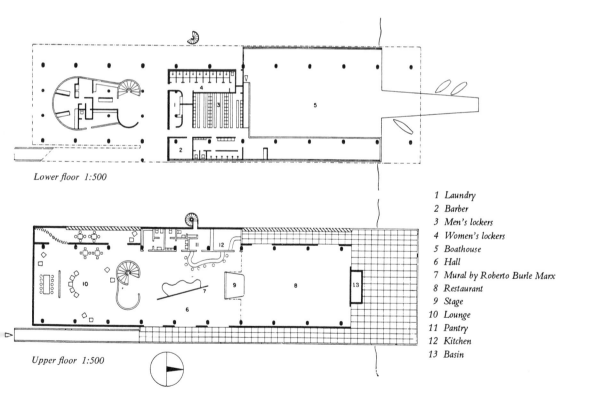

Lower floor 1:500

Upper floor 1:500

1 Laundry
2 Barber
3 Men's lockers
4 Women's lockers
5 Boathouse
6 Hall
7 Mural by Roberto Burle Marx
8 Restaurant
9 Stage
10 Lounge
11 Pantry
12 Kitchen
13 Basin

Figure 26. Yacht Club at Pampulha, 1942, plan. The club's sleek proportions and the prow-like projection of its lake façade recall the nautical imagery popularized by Le Corbusier.

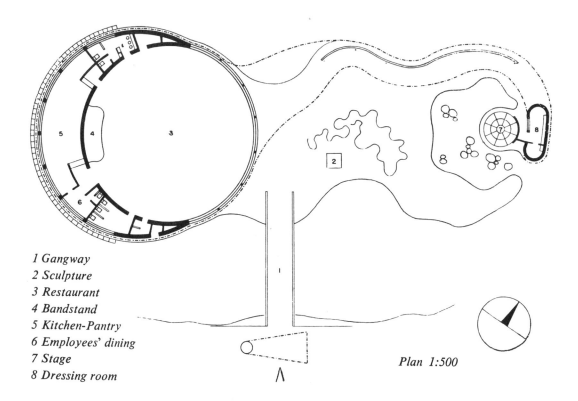

1 Gangway
2 Sculpture
3 Restaurant
4 Bandstand
5 Kitchen-Pantry
6 Employees' dining
7 Stage
8 Dressing room

Plan 1:500

Figure 27 (above). Niemeyer, Casa do Baile (restaurant and dance hall), Pampulha, 1942, plan. Structural engineer: Albino Froufe. The lines of the Casa do Baile follow the contours of the small island on which it is sited.

Figures 28–29 (opposite and above). Casa do Baile, views of restaurant and canopy. The curving concrete canopy first used here would become a major theme in Niemeyer's work. With it he defines a fluid space in a scenographic and structurally dynamic way.

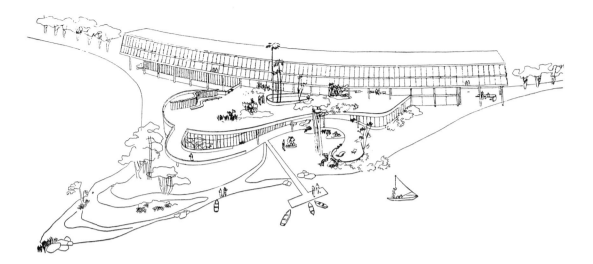

Figures 30–31. Niemeyer, project for tourist hotel, Pampulha, 1943. Structural engineer: Joaquim Cardoso. The unexecuted hotel project, intended to complete the development of Pampulha as a resort area, combines forms and themes from Niemeyer's other works there: formal contrasts, meandering canopies, integration with the landscape, and the Corbusian *jeu de rampes* and *promenade architecturale*.

Figures 32. Niemeyer, Chapel of St. Francis de Assisi, Pampulha, 1943. Structural engineer: Joaquim Cardoso. Widely acclaimed as one of Niemeyer's greatest masterpiece, the chapel expresses a Baroque unity of volume and structure through the use of a parabolic vault of reinforced concrete.

N

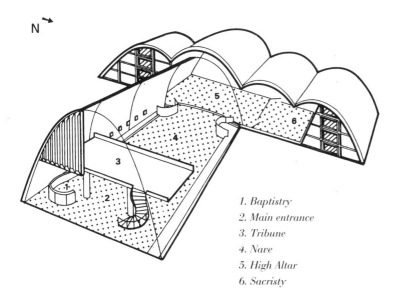

Figures 33. Chapel of St. Francis, isometric drawing. The main vault narrows toward the high altar, producing a telescoping effect that focuses the faithful on the mural of St. Francis by Candido Portinari.

1. *Baptistry*
2. *Main entrance*
3. *Tribune*
4. *Nave*
5. *High Altar*
6. *Sacristy*

The program was thoroughly Latin in its pleasure-seeking function, thoroughly Catholic in acknowledging the importance of the church within Brazilian society.

Niemeyer responded to the commission with appropriate verve and flair, taking as his compositional point of departure the natural contours of the artificial lake (figs. 19–20). The buildings at Pampulha were not conceived as an ensemble of interdependent elements, but rather as independent forms that celebrate the individual liberty of those who would enjoy them. Common to all is the commitment to indulgent freedom and an interest in formal and structural innovations. Moreover, all were conceptualized in terms of their scenographic charm within the pristine natural setting. Such natural scenographic unity was an important quality of the colonial Baroque monuments of Rio and Minas Gerais, which both Costa and Niemeyer upheld as models of good Brazilian architecture.

The masterpieces of Pampulha are the Chapel of St. Francis and the popular restaurant and dance hall, or Casa do Baile. In the latter, Niemeyer introduced the idea of a meandering concrete canopy that defines an open, natural space and that frames the visual perspectives offered by the lake. The contours of the canopy follow those of the small island on which it was designed. The dance hall was conceived as a gesture of goodwill toward those outside the circle of the Brazilian elite whose needs and interests remained otherwise unaddressed by the fashionable institutions of Pampulha's exclusive enclave. And yet it is here, in the dance hall, that we find Niemeyer at his most lyrical and "Oscaric." The forms of the dance hall illustrate Niemeyer's Baroque-inspired conception of architectural form as a setting for a multimedia sensory experience, which in this case is not only visual, but also culinary and musical.

Figures 34-35. Chapel of St. Francis, rear façade. The use of *azulejos* (the blue-and-white ceramic tile composition by Candido Portinari) provides a link to the decorative traditions of Portuguese colonial architecture.

The Chapel of St. Francis is the most innovative yet at the same time most Baroque of the buildings at Pampulha—Baroque in its sculptural conception and its spatial and structural unity, innovative for its appropriation for religious architecture of the parabola, a form that had hitherto been used only in engineering structures like Freyssinnet's airship hangar at Orly Airport in Paris. The unity of the chapel is a product of Niemeyer's use of the parabolic vault, which enabled the walls and roof to be formed as one. By telescoping the vault so that it narrows slightly as it approaches the high altar, he was able to focus the worshiper's optical and spiritual attention on the religious tenets of Franciscan piety and natural simplicity. The use of the parabola may have been inspired in part by the Orly hangar and the parabolic arch of Le Corbusier's Palace of the Soviets in Moscow (which inspired Niemeyer's use of the same motif in his national stadium project for Rio), but in terms of the sculptural conception of the whole, he was surely responding as well to Brazil's natural parabolas—the mountains of Minas Gerais and Rio. Sugar Loaf has been to Niemeyer what Mt. Sainte Victoire was to Cézanne: an image of nature's permanence, a haunting formal and spiritual presence that would continue to inspire his art, sometimes perhaps unconsciously.

In designing the chapel and Pampulha's other monuments, Niemeyer benefited from the collaboration of a talented group of colleagues—from the structural engineer Joaquim Cardozo and the landscape architect Roberto Burle Marx to the painter-muralist Candido Portinari, who was responsible for the mural of St. Francis in the church's high altar and for the *azulejo* (ceramic tile) design that graces the church's rear façade with the same bright colors that decorate the interiors of colonial Baroque churches like N. S. da Glória do Outeiro in Rio.

Niemeyer has habitually used *azulejos* as a decorative element to give his architecture color and Brazilian flavor. We see them as well on the exterior of a small theater with twin auditoriums he designed for a site immediately adjacent to the Ministry of Health and Education Building in Rio (figs. 36–38). For this unexecuted project, Niemeyer created an organic and smoothly undulating form that contrasts dramatically with the rigid and erect posture of the Corbusian slab behind. This is perhaps the most outspoken example of one of Niemeyer's favorite games—that of formal oppositions, here suggesting a new Brazilian aesthetic identity in opposition to the hard and straight (male) forms of the European architect. For here, the wavelike contours of this biomorphic building echo those of Niemeyer's drawings of the female sunbather on Copacabana (figs. 39 and 40).

Niemeyer's violent oppositions, his biomorphic forms, and their natural sources of inspiration invite a comparison with the Surrealist search for the fantastic and the automatic. Niemeyer's design method is of course never purely automatic, a technique explored by the Surrealists; it combines both

Figure 36. Niemeyer, photomontage of unexecuted 1948 project for theater with twin auditoriums, adjoining the Ministry of Education and Health Building, Rio. After Pampulha, Niemeyer continued to explore vaulted and dynamically curved structures such as the one shown here, with a tendency toward more biomorphic forms that contrasted with the hard lines of European modernism and pushed concrete to its tactile limits.

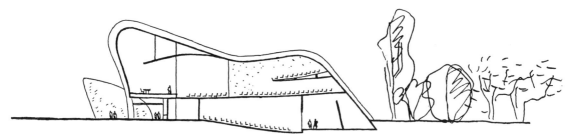

Figure 37. Project for ministry theater, section. The twin auditoriums featured dramatically cantilevered galleries and suspended ceilings.

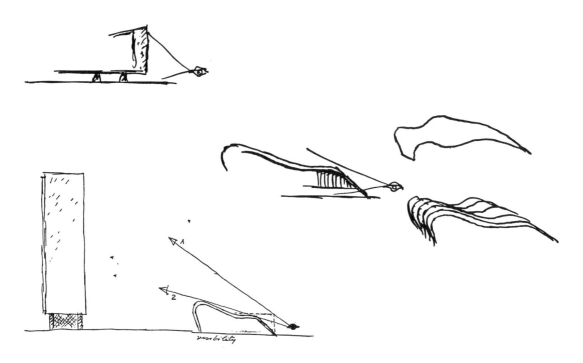

Figure 38. Project for ministry theater, preliminary drawings. The sketches reveal Niemeyer's interest in visibility, sight lines, and the dynamic relationship between the contrasting rectilinear and curvilinear forms.

Figures 39–40. Niemeyer, sketches of Brazilian women on the beach. The contours of the sun-bather's backside suggest the biomorphic curves of the ministry theater.

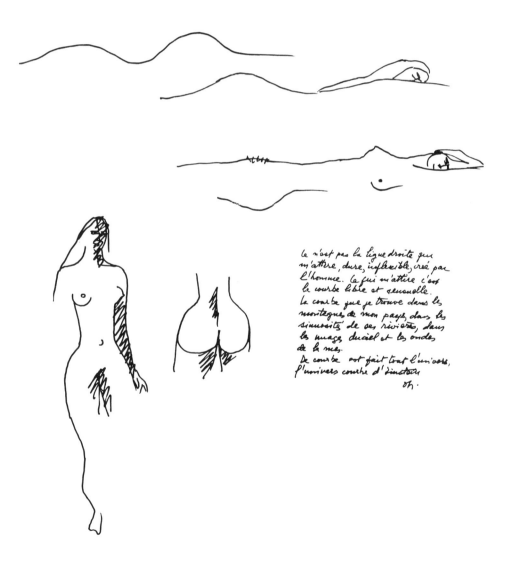

Ce n'est pas la ligne droite qui
m'attire, dure, inflexible, créé par
l'homme. Ce qui m'attire c'est
la courbe libre et sensuelle.
La courbe que je trouve dans les
montagnes de mon pays, dans les
sinuosité de ses rivières, dans
les nuages du ciel et les ondes
de la mer.
De courbe est fait tout l'univers,
l'univers courbe d'Einstein
oh.

the rational and irrational. But the rational side of his approach—his preliminary analysis of the program and the resources available, not to mention his contextual determinism (the belief that architecture is fundamentally conditioned by the society and environment that produce it)—has misled some observers to dismiss any connections with the Surrealists. But Niemeyer himself confesses a personal taste for Surrealist sculpture and the mysterious landscapes of Yves Tanguy and Jean Carzou, and his late work reveals affinities with the fluid compositions and biomorphic forms of Joan Miró.

Central to Surrealism, the late work of Le Corbusier, and the free-form work of Niemeyer is their poetic base. Niemeyer's rich capacity for visual poetry, however, transcends the Corbusian discourse in seeking a more vital relationship between the language of the plastic arts and the language of poetry, a relationship that is not just a matter of illustrating the latter by the former. Niemeyer has both imagined and created an architecture that transforms poetry into something that can be seen and touched. His method is thus akin to that decribed by René Magritte, who wrote: "It is a matter of imagining images whose poetry restores to what is known that which is absolutely unknown or unknowable."[29]

The Surrealist quest is most typically a Freudian psychological exploration of the treasures hidden in the human mind. Such matters are pertinent to architecture because, as Le Corbusier reminds us, "the exterior is always an interior."[30] The work of Niemeyer is likewise concerned with dreams and inner secrets that are revealed or disguised in the forms of the artist. Surrealism and Niemeyer's architecture are both based on an acceptance of the world of dreams and inner desires, sexual and spiritual, which the artist seeks to liberate. Niemeyer achieves this personal liberation in part through his architecture, in part through his writing, and especially through his creation of a convenient "other," an alter ego with whom he maintains an ongoing dialogue on secret matters that interest them both. The pervasiveness of this tropical Jekyll and Hyde syndrome even led Niemeyer to write a book on the subject, a poetic retrospective called *Meu Sósia e Eu* (*My Double and I*).[31] Niemeyer's "double" is above all a creative vehicle he uses for talking to himself, as well as to us, about "forbidden things" that "he" likes:

He likes beauty. Women fascinate him and nature impresses him. We have many things in common. If I start to design a project, he takes me by the hand, leading me in ecstasy towards new shapes, curved and unexpected as we prefer them. Memories of our country, its mountains, the sensual curves of a beautiful woman. But he is lascivious. If a woman approaches, he starts to insinuate forbidden things. . . . Purer than I—he does not know society's prejudices—he suggests impossible things. Yet, it is not difficult to lead him towards social problems. His fraternal pattern helps. Like this we go, hand in hand, dreaming about a better world.[32]

As this passage suggests, Niemeyer's utopian dreams of a better world are firmly rooted in "memories of our country." An important element of the Luso-Brazilian lust for life is the *saudade*, the longing and deep nostalgia for home and lost worlds, for the primitive and the past—all of which Niemeyer explores with an eye to the possibility of a future Eden. His lost world is that of the mythical paradise of Brazil, before European exploitation and industrial development. His Proustian search for lost times focuses on Rio before it was spoiled by hideous overbuilding, on the evenings spent with friends, barhopping in the Lapa district, but his true paradise is a retreat to the pristine forests and hills of the Brazilian interior—and above all, a personal retreat into the past of his youth, when he was surrounded by his family, with all the maternal protection and paternal security it provided. Such memories, the stuff of his dreams, inform his architecture in a subtle but important way. They conditioned his decision to erect the several houses he built for himself, which reflected the quest for domestic security in a world whose traditional social relations were being disrupted by the forces of industrialization and urban dislocation; his decision to build a family retreat at Mendes; his effort to find a nurturing force in nature and to create a natural architecture that is best illustrated by the house he built for himself on the Canoas road, high up on the mountainous outskirts of Rio's southern zone. But the Mendes House, Niemeyer's Combray, is the focus of special memories that anticipate an architecture to come, for there, "in the old walls corroded by dampness, old and sweet memories were left behind." He recalls his Aunt Alzira's old colonial house, "all whitewashed with blue windows and an enormous roof, in the Portuguese style."[33] His art of enormous white forms was at least in part an attempt to recapture this lost but precious past.

Niemeyer's longing for the past takes the form of a symbiotic identification of the life of the artist, the life of the place, and the natural forms of architecture. This identification has involved the architect's fixation on certain objects of nature, both general and specific—the beach and Sugar Loaf. But the huge granite boulder that forms the centerpiece of his house at Canoas (figs. 41–44) would seem the supreme example of a Surrealist natural object in his architecture. Canoas is also proof of Le Corbusier's observation that "passion can create drama out of inert stone."[34] Like André Breton, who wrote *Les langues des pierres*, Niemeyer too saw in the mineral kingdom a poetic domain of signs and indications. The interpretation of the stone and other found objects satisfies and develops the poetic sense, which man must cultivate. Breton suggested that "stones—particularly hard stones

Figure 41. Niemeyer, architect's house at Canoas, Rio de Janeiro, 1953, general view. The essence of the Canoas house is the concrete canopy whose curving contours seem to have been cut out of the surrounding mountainside. Here Niemeyer sought to neutralize the distinction between architecture and the landscape in the ultimate "natural" house.

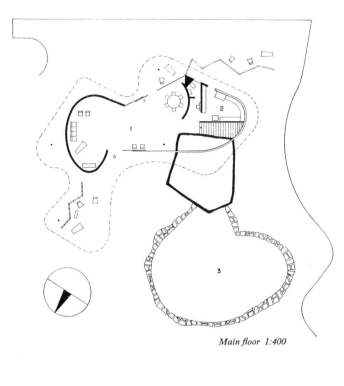

Figure 42. House at Canoas, plan. Niemeyer's house, the purest example of free-form modernism in domestic architecture, derives its expressive power from the fluidity of its spaces and the attention given to the natural elements of the site: stone, water, and vegetation. The garden was landscaped by Roberto Burle Marx.

Main floor 1:400

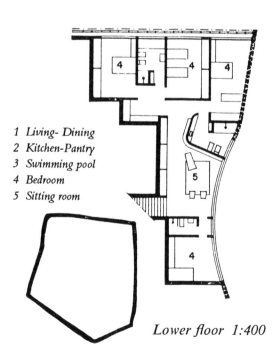

1 *Living- Dining*
2 *Kitchen-Pantry*
3 *Swimming pool*
4 *Bedroom*
5 *Sitting room*

Lower floor 1:400

Figure 43. House at Canoas, view of granite boulder. The centerpiece of the composition is a huge outcropping of Carioca granite. Niemeyer has created an escapist's dream house that is nonetheless firmly anchored in the geological reality of his native Rio.

Figure 44. House at Canoas, view through living room. The walls of the house are almost entirely glazed, so that the interior is surrounded by the tropical landscape. Niemeyer let nature be his interior decorator.

[like the Canoas boulder]—go on talking to those who wish to hear them. They speak to each listener according to his capabilities; through what each listener knows, they instruct him in what he aspires to know."[35] Such speaking forms are typical of Niemeyer's visual poetry.

The Italian critic Ernesto Rogers, though critical of the "Romantic" aspect of Niemeyer's unprecedented natural house, clearly "heard" the language of forms of the Canoas boulder and its architectural progeny:

I doubt that I shall ever forget that scene: the sun was just dipping below the horizon, leaving us in a dark sea of orange, violet, green, and indigo. The house repeated the themes of that orgiastic countryside (incense and the hum of insects); a vast rhapsody beginning in the roof vibrated down the walls and their niches to finish in the pool, where the water, instead of being neatly dammed up, freely spread along the rocks of a kind of forest pool.[36]

The sensual discovery of the rock and the house that springs forth from it in a poetic microcosm of the Brazilian landscape reflects the artist's desire to find permanent integration via architecture within that landscape. In the words of Giorgio de Chirico: "By the act of discovery we make life possible, in the sense that we reconcile it with its mother, Eternity."[37] As Niemeyer later wrote: "In the attraction that nature awakened in us, there was something that reminded us of integration and eternity."[38]

Niemeyer's quest for eternity is an even more important theme in the work he produced after his first trip to Europe in 1954. The monuments of Europe impressed him with a sense of symbolic permanence that pervades his project for the Museum of Modern Art in Caracas and his more important creations in the new Brazilian capital. For the Caracas museum (figs. 45–47), he designed a pure pyramidal form of classical derivation in which the stable structural orthodoxies of Europe are turned upside down. This was perhaps the most dramatic statement of his revolt against structural norms. Had the musuem been executed, it would have proven the Corbusian dictum that "the laws of gravity, of statics and of dynamics, impose themselves by a reductio ad absurdum: everything must hold together or it will collapse."[39] Such a theorem applies well to Niemeyer's architecture and to the socioeconomic situation in Brazil, both of which often stradle the fine line between stability and collapse. The art of living dangerously, the essence of *jeito*, is the stuff of Rio and Niemeyer's best architecture.

Niemeyer's best free-form architecture is a festival of the imagination that participates in the larger Surrealist conquest of the marvelous. His most provocative work fits Alexandrian's description of Surrealist art as "not so much the description of the impossible as the evocation of the possible, supplemented by desire and dream."[40]

Figure 45. Niemeyer, project for Museum of Modern Art, Caracas, 1954–55, model (unexecuted). Designed following Niemeyer's first trip to Europe in 1954, the museum reflects the architect's new interest in pure geometric forms in free space and his search for a more complete integration of monumental form, dynamic structure, and symbolic content.

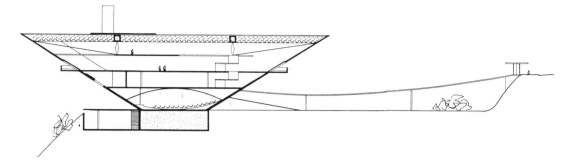

Figure 46. Project for Caracas museum, section. Niemeyer proposed the inverted pyramid form to maximize exhibition space and natural lighting for the museum.

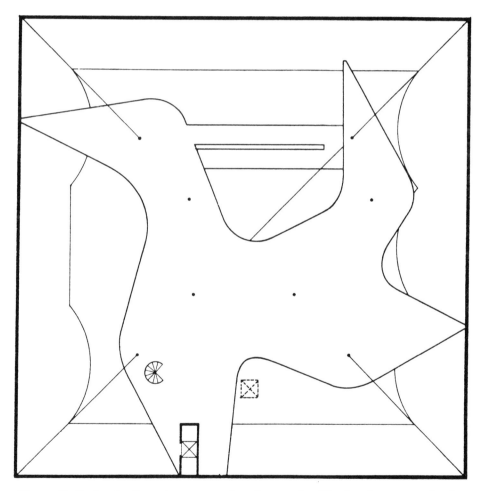

Figure 47. Project for Caracas musuem, plan of mezzanine. The free-form mezzanine floor was to be suspended from the roof, thus freeing the main gallery from structural supports and providing 13,100 square feet of exhibition space.

We see this not only in Canoas, but especially in Brasília and the work subsequent to it: both Surrealism and Niemeyer's architecture strive for something that "cannot accurately be described as fantasy, but as a superior reality, in which all the contradictions which afflict humanity are resolved as in a dream."[41] In Brasília, Niemeyer's superior reality is one based on an insistent unity that partakes of the spirit of classical permanence—a surreal classicism that synthesizes the sublime and the beautiful.

The quest for permanence in the face of political vicissitudes—a quest that characterized the Surrealist attitude toward revolution—is also evident in Niemeyer's political outlook, especially in his dialectical materialism. Both Niemeyer and the Surrealists wanted to advance the cause of the proletariat against capitalist society, but neither was prepared to sacrifice the creation of art and the freeing of the imagination. Gradually the insistence on revolution was replaced in Surrealism by an appeal to magic, as expressed in Breton's *L'Art magique* (1957). Alexandrian points out: "Revolution and magic were the two values which surrealism used to conceal its unconfessed raison d'être, which was to make a religion out of poetic inspiration." These two values are a constant dichotomy in Surrealist thought, whose contradictions "are a direct result of the impossibility of reconciling them."[42] Niemeyer's work sought aesthetically to harmonize revolution and magic.

In his masterpiece, the architecture of Brasília, structural and formal magic is the means to both aesthetic revolution and spiritual redemption. A city of hope and ultimately of illusion, Brasília confronts us with a number of paradoxes. In terms of Niemeyer's development as an artist, the city represents the paradox of increased formal discipline and the concurrent achievement of a free space for the imagination based on the revolt against structural orthodoxies expressed in the Caracas museum project.

Appointed director of Brasília's works by his long-time friend and patron Juscelino Kubitschek, then the president of the republic, Niemeyer enjoyed a virtual carte blanche over artistic decision making in the creation of the city's major monuments. But in the face of widespread public criticism of Kubitschek's defiance of the Brazilian law that called for open competitions for public buildings, the project for the city's master plan was opened to a national competition held on March 16, 1957. Niemeyer, a member of the jury, nonetheless retained considerable influence over the final decision that awarded the project to his mentor Lúcio Costa.

Costa's plan was based on a Corbusian "primordial axis" intersected by another, curving axis to define the form of an airplane or a bird in flight (figs. 48 and 49). Niemeyer's scenographic conceptualization of the city's monuments within Costa's pilot plan similarly reflected a Corbusian perspective (figs. 50–52): "A bird's eye view such as is given by a plan on a drawing board is not how the axes are seen; they are seen from the ground, the beholder standing up and looking in front of him."[43] But the developmental priorities of President Kubitschek's regime ("Fifty years of progress in five") placed a premium on speed, of the futuristic sort that valued aviation over the pedestrian. Brasília's multilane highways resemble runways; and Niemeyer's architectural creations make conscious use of the metaphor of flight, emphasizing a magical weightlessness that was to symbolize the miracle of Brazilian national progress in Brasília.

Brasília's magical structures reflect Niemeyer's rebellion against structural norms (fig. 53) and his interest in creating new forms of rich sculptural effect. The paradox of the Alvorada Palace (Palace of Dawn); (figs. 54–57), the isolated residence of the

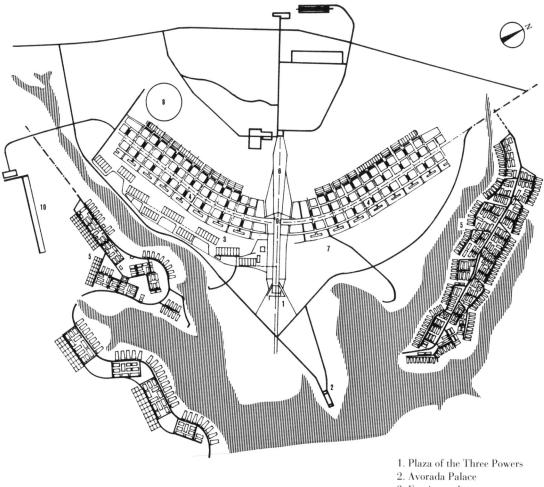

1. Plaza of the Three Powers
2. Avorada Palace
3. Foreign embassys
4. Inner residential zone
5. Outer residential zone
6. Main axis

Figure 48. Lúcio Costa, plan of Brasília, 1956. Costa conceived the plan of Brasília in terms of two monumental axes intersecting to resemble a fuselage and wings.

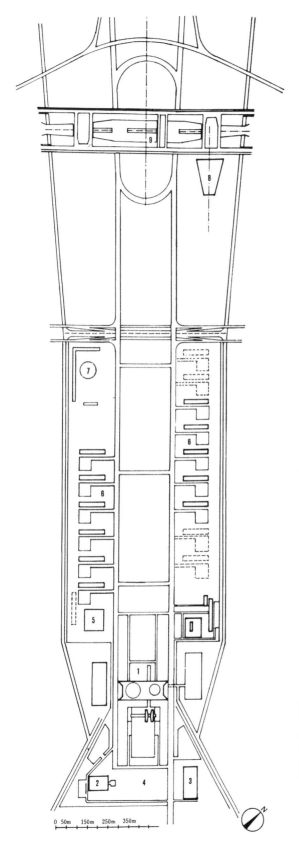

1. Congress Complex
2. Supreme Court
3. Planalto Palace
4. Plaza of the Three Powers
5. Foreign Office (Itamaraty)
6. Ministry buildings
7. Cathedral
8. Theater
9. Main traffic interchange

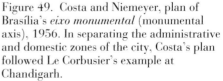

Figure 49. Costa and Niemeyer, plan of Brasília's *eixo monumental* (monumental axis), 1956. In separating the administrative and domestic zones of the city, Costa's plan followed Le Corbusier's example at Chandigarh.

Figure 50. Costa (plan) and Niemeyer (buildings), view of Brasília's monumental axis toward the Congress complex. Niemeyer conceived of his buildings as monumental urban sculptures that would complement Costa's plan, function as urban scenography, and symbolize Brazilian modernity.

Figure 51. Niemeyer, Congress complex, Brasília, 1958, with senate chambers, administration towers, and chamber of deputies. Niemeyer's compositions at Brasília were based on the play of formal contrasts—curved versus straight— and on the inversion of conventional volumes anticipated in the Caracas musuem project.

Figure 52. Niemeyer, Praça dos Três Poderes (Plaza of the Three Powers), Brasília, 1958, looking toward the administration towers and the Museum of the City of Brasília. The Plaza of the Three Powers lies at the head of the monumental axis and links the major government buildings. Niemeyer sought to capture something of the monumental grandeur and dignified unity of the great civic squares of Europe.

president and the first of Niemeyer's palaces to be erected, is that its innovative form is a product of Niemeyer's evolution of a new parabolic structural element that is in fact nonstructural. The curving colonnade of the Alvorada is not a colonnade at all, but an inverted parabolic arcade supported by low-springing arches that barely touch the ground. The façade thus appears elegantly weightless. The main volume of the building, a glass box positioned between two projecting floor slabs connected by the arcade, appears to float above the reflecting pool in front of the palace. But this is only an illusion: the box is firmly anchored to the ground via a solid basement that is hidden by the colonnade, which also obscures the internal and external supports sustaining the floor slabs. The illusion is completed by the image of the façade in the reflecting pool, in which the inverted arcade is turned right-side up. Niemeyer's creative manipulation of the structural theme of the classical arcade into a series of inverted parabolas with little or no structural function

Figure 53. Niemeyer, Museum of the City of Brasília, 1958. Designed to commemorate the founding of the city and the patronage of President Juscelino Kubitschek (whose bust is attached to the facade), Niemeyer's museum is a dramatically cantilevered structure that attests to the daring of Brazilian modernizers and the powers of reinforced concrete.

Figure 54. Niemeyer, Alvorada Palace, Brasília, 1957, main façade. Structural engineer: Joaquim Cardoso. The colonnade of inverted parabolas that support the gallery of the presidential residence became a national symbol of the city's architecture. Niemeyer here created a modernized version of the traditional palace theme.

Figure 55. Alvorada Palace, entrance vestibule. The palace's interiors, designed by Niemeyer's daughter, Ana Maria, combined precious materials and mirrored surfaces, creating the impression of a modern Versailles.

Figure 56. Alvorada Palace, view toward garden. The palace is set on a vast landscaped garden featuring sculptures by Maria Martins and Alfredo Ceschiatti.

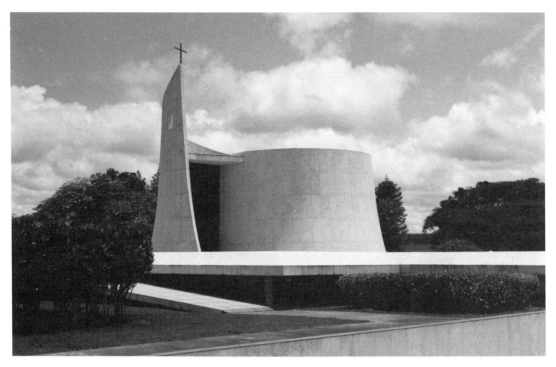

Figure 57. Niemeyer, Alvorada Palace Chapel, Brasília, 1958. Niemeyer's presidential chapel was inspired by the organic form of Le Corbusier's chapel at Ronchamp.

reflects his Surrealistic approach to the classical and the conventional.

Niemeyer's palaces evoke the possibility of human spiritual redemption through otherworldly images of the dreamlike, the ethereal, and the fluid. Flights of formal fantasy, conceived in the monumental scenographic terms we see in the Alvorada, became the basis for his synthesis of the surreal, the classical, and the Baroque. The feather-light structures of Niemeyer's government palaces (figs. 58–60), perched magically on the ground, are to be seen as metaphors of modernity and a means to the spiritual uplifting of mankind. Taking as his point of departure the model of the Greek temple, Niemeyer designed the Planalto Palace and the Supreme Court with these considerations in mind:

When thinking out the forms for these palaces, I also bore in mind the kind of mood they would impart to the Plaza of the Three Powers. . . . I visualized it with a richness of forms, dreams, and poetry, like the mysterious paintings by Carzou, new forms, startling visitors by their lightness and creative liberty; forms that were not anchored to the earth rigidly and statically, but that uplifted the Palaces as if to suspend them, white and ethereal, in the endless nights of the highlands; surprising and breathtaking forms that would lift the visitor, if only for a few brief instants, above the difficult and at times overwhelming problems which life poses for all of us.[44]

The architecture of Brasília is thus rooted in a fundamentally Surrealist project: the attempt to call into question the objects and conventions of the everyday and the commonplace through deliberate juxtaposition with the extraordinary and the marvelous. The futuristic complex of the national legislature, with its fantastic formal inversions of concave, convex, and rectilinear shapes, thus derives its symbolic meaning from the inevitable comparison of its daring forms with the mundane

Figure 58. Niemeyer, Supreme Court, Brasília, 1958, main façade. Niemeyer wrapped an International Style box with a series of elegant curving supports that give the building a feeling of ethereal grace. The palaces of Brasília recall the prototype of the Greco-Roman temple, but their floating and ethereal qualities evoke the surreal as well as the classical.

Figures 59. Niemeyer, Planalto Palace, Brasília, 1958, main façade. Niemeyer unified the Planalto Palace and the Supreme Court across the square by using the same curving colonnaded structure for both. He wanted to create the impression that the buildings were as "light as a feather," barely touching the ground.

Figure 60. Planalto Palace, showing Bruno Giorgi's sculpture *The Warriors* in the foreground.

International Style slabs of the ministry buildings that line the monumental axis. The most important among the ministry functions, however, the Ministries of Justice (fig. 61) and Foreign Relations (fig. 62), take up again the classical theme of the palaces—in a way that dignifies their functions and sets them apart within Brasília's hierarchy of forms.

The graceful curving forms of the capital complex, with its bowl-shaped volume suggestive of a flying saucer and a futuristic flight path, were intended to function not only symbolically but also scenographically—as visual framers of the natural and man-made objects of the cityscape. In Brasília, Niemeyer sought a poetic interaction between architecture and the vast skies of the highland plains, an interaction that would enable the spirit to soar to new heights of imagination and spiritual fulfillment. With his head and his heart in the clouds, he finds the fantasies he always seeks in a narrative poem titled "Clouds":

Figure 61. Niemeyer, Ministry of Justice, Brasília, 1962. Niemeyer inserted waterspouts beneath the arches of the facade to create a sense of surprise and the unexpected.

Figure 62. Niemeyer, Ministry of
Foreign Relations (Palácio de
Itamaraty), Brasília, 1962. Niemeyer
rendered round arches in brute con-
crete to give the building a powerful,
Romanizing effect. There is a garden
on the roof terrace by Roberto Burle
Marx.

"Whenever I traveled by car to Brasília, my pas-
time was to watch the clouds in the sky. How many
unexpected things they suggest! Sometimes they
are huge and mysterious cathedrals, Exupéry's
cathedrals no doubt; other times, terrible warriors,
Roman chariots riding through the air, or unknown
monsters running through the winds at full tilt, and
more often, because I was always searching for
them, beautiful and vaporous women reclining on
the clouds, smiling at me from infinite spaces."

Niemeyer describes how suddenly the shifting
winds of the high plains turn the dream into a neb-
ulous nightmare, destroying his fantasy:

"Soon everything was transformed: the cathedrals vanished in a white fog, the warriors became
an endless carnival procession; the monsters hid in
dark caves only to emerge even more furious, while
the women began to fade and spread apart, transformed into birds or black serpents."

To freeze the dream and thus make it permanent
is the architect's elusive project. But the image, like

nature, space, and life itself, remains fluid and changing:

"Many times I thought of photographing all this, so precise were the pictures which I saw. I never did it." Instead he keeps looking at the clouds, trying to decipher them "as if searching for a good and expected message." One day, the vision appears again:

"On that day, though, the vision was even more incredible. It was a beautiful woman, rosy as a Renoir painting. The oval face, the full breasts, the smooth belly, and the long legs interlaced in the white clouds in the sky. I watched her, in complete rapture, afraid she might suddenly fade away. But on that summer afternoon the wind was probably listening to me and she remained there for a long time, looking at me from a distance, as if inviting me to come up and frolic with her among the clouds. But what I feared had to happen. Little by little my girlfriend started fading away, her arms extending with despair, her breasts flying apart as if separating from her body, her long legs twisting into spirals, as if she did not want to leave that place. Only the eyes continued to stare at me, getting bigger and bigger, full of surprise and sadness, then a larger cloud, dense and black, took her away from me. I kept watching her, disturbed, seeing her struggle with the clouds which surrounded her, seeing her torn by the winds which took her apart mercilessly."

In the end, it is not just her image and her love that elude the poet architect, but life itself:

"I felt how that perverse metamorphosis was similar to our own destiny: we are obliged to be born, grow, struggle, die, and disappear forever, as it was with that beautiful figure of woman."[45]

Niemeyer's art, particularly in Brasília, is a quest for eternity, a means to express permanence in the face of change and dissolution. Like Sartre and Lacan, Niemeyer bemoans the absurd tragedy of human existence. The only certainties are mortality and the need for a heroic, permanent, and poetic architecture in which mankind can find some form of redemption in the face of the personal losses, political turmoil, and social injustices of modern history, in the face of a tragic destiny he cannot change. If this fatalistic view recalls Le Corbusier's "tragic vision," it also reminds us of André Malraux's view of man's conquest of destiny through art—the highest form of social action. Though the result is sometimes criticized as self-indulgent and arbitrary formalism, the quest for beauty in Niemeyer's art—as in that of Malraux and Le Corbusier—is ultimately a spiritual quest, a search through art for something that, in Le Corbusier's words, is "deep within us and beyond our senses, a resonance, a sort of sounding-board which begins to vibrate . . . an indefinable trace of the Absolute which lies in the depths of our being."[40]

Niemeyer's search for intimacy with the divine is most powerfully expressed in his cathedral, the masterpiece of Brasília (figs. 63–67). Here Niemeyer achieves a unity of form, volume, structure, and religious symbolism by defining the building in terms of the volumetric essence created by its structural elements. Their spiky upper portions also function symbolically to remind us of the crown of the Queen of Heaven and the crown of thorns in the Passion of Christ. Sixteen boomerang-shaped ribs, secured at their base by a seventy-meter ring of concrete and at the top only by a thin concrete slab, reach for the heavens "like a cry of faith and hope." The volume thus defined by the ribs and glazed panels between them is a circular hyperboloid of remarkable purity and grace. The cathedral's equation of the structural skeleton with the building itself is the most daring example of Niemeyer's dictum "when the structure is done the building is finished." Moreover, it seemed that Niemeyer had imagined a structure that modern technology could not implement: the glazing of the irregularly shaped interstices between the ribs

Figures 63–64 (opposite page). Niemeyer, Cathedral of Brasília, 1959. The essence of the building is the series of sixteen structural ribs resembling boomerangs, brought together at the top and held in place by a concrete ring at the base. Niemeyer wanted to evoke the structural magic and spiritual power of the Gothic cathedral. The ribs, originally of exposed concrete, were recently treated with a special white paint to preserve the material and accentuate color contrasts. The bell tower and baptistry stand independent of the main structure.

Figure 65. Cathedral of Brasília, entrance, with statues of the apostles by Ceschiatti. Niemeyer designed the access to the cathedral through a dark underground corridor to create in the visitor a sense of surprise caused by the contrast between its darkness and the colorful light of the sanctuary.

Figure 66–67 (left and opposite). Cathedral of Brasília, interiors. The recently replaced stained glass is by Marianne Peretti, the angels by Ceschiatti.

represented a formidable technical challenge, one that was met only after a long period of analysis and consultation with glass manufacturers. The replacement of the original glass with new panels by the same designer, Marianne Peretti, has enhanced the luminosity and coloristic effect of the whole.

But the magic of the cathedral is as much spatial as structural and technical. The entrance to the sanctuary, through a descending ramp framed by statues of the apostles by Alfredo Ceschiatti, was designed by Niemeyer to accentuate the contrast between the darkness of the underground passage and the uplifting light of the sanctuary, thus providing an architectural promenade that parallels the itinerary of the human soul en route to redemption. The cathedral reflects Niemeyer's conception of architecture as a utopian means of spiritually uplifting the masses through the play of light on forms and the interpenetration of space through a magical structure.

III. THE UTOPIAN IMPULSE

I believed as I still do, that unless there is a just distribution of wealth reaching all sectors of the populace, the basic objective of architecture, that is its social base, would be sacrificed, and our role as architects only relegated to satisfying the whims of the wealthy.

—Oscar Niemeyer

Form is a mystery, which eludes definition, but makes man feel good in a way quite unlike social aid.

—Alvar Aalto, 1955

The utopian dream of a more just society for the people of Latin America has been a major, if somewhat paradoxical, theme in Niemeyer's career. Brasília epitomizes Niemeyer's effort to create through architecture a brave new world—one that turns its back on the past to project a future based on a Corbusian vision of a rational, mechanized society. The failures of this project have been widely criticized: the promised land has yet to deliver its promises to the working-class masses who live in permanent poverty in the rings of shantytowns surrounding the monumental core. Saddened by Brasília's social failures and the subversion of his communist social vision by the unrelenting interests of capitalist development, Niemeyer insists that he never claimed that architecture could create a utopia of justice and equality for the masses. Instead, he recasts in more cautious terms the Corbusian notion of architecture as an instrument for the improvement of society (an idea expressed in the slogan "architecture or revolution"): while the architect may express his social idealism by seeking to project through architectural form a society that does not yet exist, he is convinced nonetheless that basic social change must come first.

Implicit in Niemeyer's attitude are two possible courses of action. The first is to promote change through direct political involvement, while at the same time continuing to perform the crucial role of the architect—to create forms. The second is to strive to design works that call for change, reflect the plight of the masses, or serve as an escape valve for socioeconomic frustrations. During the post-Brasília phase of his career, from the early 1960s to the present, Niemeyer has pursued both of these options, while at the same time attempting to refine and perfect the structural and formal innovations of the first half of his career. What he has sought most consistently is an "obstinate utopia of beauty" that would elevate men out of their quotidian turmoils.

A member of the Brazilian Communist Party since 1945, Niemeyer was forced into exile after the rightist military coup of 1964. During the years of Brazil's repressive dictatorial regime (1964–85), his office in Rio was ransacked and the publication of his journal *Módulo* was suspended. He was detained and interrogated by the military police on several occasions. "What is it you communists want?" they demanded. "To change society," he responded. But with his patronage undercut and his dream of a just society for Brazil shattered by the dictatorship, Niemeyer sought work abroad—in Europe, Africa, and the Middle East.

In terms of form, Niemeyer's post-Brasília work reflects two general tendencies: (1) the elaboration and refinement of previous formal innovations; and (2) the development of his thinking about city planning and the urban ensemble. The twenty-year period after 1962 was one of creative experimentation that set up the final, Brazilian phase of his career in which these two tendencies are synthesized in his masterpiece, the Memorial da América Latina in São Paulo (1989). The curving, free-form layout of the memorial is anticipated in the permanent ensemble that Niemeyer designed for the

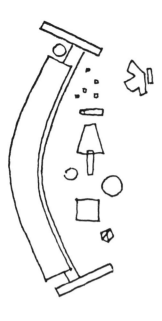

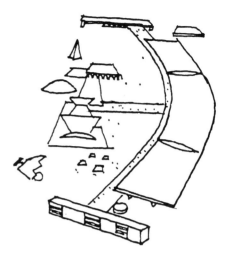

Figure 68. Niemeyer, International Exposition, Tripoli, Lebanon, 1962, plan and sketch. The complex illustrates the evolution of Niemeyer's free-form mode on the spatial level of the urban ensemble: a Surrealistic carnival of forms.

International Exposition in Tripoli, Lebanon, in 1962 (fig. 68). The visual dynamism of the complex derives from the contrast between a central group of pavilions conceived as pure geometric volumes (cylinder, pyramid, etc.), on the one hand, and the sprawling curvilinear contour of a concrete canopy, on the other. This canopy recalls the one Niemeyer used to connect the pavilions at Ibirapuera Park in São Paulo, designed between 1951 and 1954 on the occasion of the city's fourth centennial celebration.

The free forms of the Tripoli exposition are further elaborated in the project for a new capital complex for Algiers, commissioned by the Algerian dictator, Boumedienne, in 1968. Niemeyer's plan combined functional zoning with a sensitivity to the Arab pattern of spontaneous or "organic" urban development. Its focal point was a monumental civic plaza defined by government ministries and a council chamber with an ogival arcade—an abstract evocation of the Islamic, but one firmly rooted in the formal experiments of the palaces of

Figure 69. Niemeyer, project for civic square for new Algerian capital, near Algiers, 1968, model on photo-montage. Niemeyer's proposed government buildings (foreground) recall the fluid forms of bedouin tents.

Brasília. Niemeyer also planned a monument to the Algerian Revolution in the form of an inclined obelisk (fig. 69) and a floating mosque whose supports again recalled the structural innovations of Brasília.

Although the capital project was not carried out, a related commission for a new campus for the University of Constantine, Algeria, was (1969–77). The university (fig. 70) demonstrates Niemeyer's attempt to use free-form design in a project that emphasized the consolidation of volumes and the centralization of academic functions.

Niemeyer's European works reflect his refinement of the themes and forms developed in his projects of the 1950s and 1960s. For instance, the new headquarters of the Mondadori Publishing Company (fig. 71), erected between 1968 and

Figure 70. Niemeyer, University of
Constantine, Algeria, 1969–77, general view. Niemeyer consolidated the
multiple functions of the university
into a few basic free-form structures.
(Courtesy Michel Moch.)

Figure 71. Niemeyer, Mondadori Publishing Company, Milan, 1968–75, façade. Niemeyer created a
rhythmic variation on the theme of the Itamaraty Palace in Brasília. (Courtesy Michel Moch.)

Figure 72. Niemeyer, French Communist Party Headquarters, Paris, 1965–80. The architect created dynamic spatial and sculptural effects despite the tight and irregular Parisian site.

1975 on the outskirts of Milan, derives from the Itamaraty Palace in Brasília, with its imposing façade of tall Roman-style arches in front of a reflecting pool. Here, however, the arches are given varying widths, and the result is an entirely new free-form rhythm of great structural dynamism. In the French Communist Party Headquarters in Paris (fig. 72), commissioned by the party chairman in 1965 and begun in 1967, Niemeyer set the senate dome of Brasília in front of the meandering slab of his earlier Copan Building in São Paulo (1951–57), but on a smaller scale and with greater attention to the compact urban lot. Through skillful grading of the irregular site, the main block was erected so that it appears to float above the ground-level terrace, but without the use of pilotis. As in the Cathedral of Brasília, Niemeyer "buried" the major functional spaces—the auditorium for party assemblies (expressed by the dome) and an adjacent workers' hall—in order to create a sculptural event based on the juxtaposition of objects of contrasting surfaces, colors, and materials (smooth black glass and rough-textured white concrete). The theme of formal contrasts is taken up again in the Workers' Hall (Bourse de Travail) in Bobigny, France (1972–80), but here the auditorium is expressed by an even freer, more sculpturally expressive shell-like structure of striated concrete (figs. 73 and 74).

In Niemeyer's European work, this tendency toward a greater sculptural dynamism of form culminates in the Maison de la Culture in Le Havre, erected between 1972 and 1982 (figs. 75–78). Its program reflects the architect's utopian interest in the concept of "public culture" promoted by André Malraux, de Gaulle's Minister of Culture, who envisioned the cultural center as a democratic institution open to all. The complex contains exhibition spaces, offices, and a state-of-the-art theater—all positioned around a sunken plaza with shops, a nursery school, and open spaces for promenades and gatherings. Niemeyer's innovative and highly sculptural use of concrete in this complex must be seen in the context of the architecture that surrounds it, that of Auguste Perret, the "magician of reinforced concrete." It was Perret who reconstructed Le Havre in his sober style of concrete classicism after the city had been devastated by extensive German bombing during World War II. In echoing the "cooling tower" form of Le Corbusier's Parliament Building in Chandigarh, Niemeyer's new magic, the complex hyperboloidal and paraboloidal forms at Le Havre, demonstrates the tremendous progress made in concrete construction techniques since Perret's time.

Several of Niemeyer's major Brazilian works of the early 1980s reflect his continuing interest in creating through architecture a more egalitarian public culture for his fellow countrymen. In the Centros Integrados de Educação Pública (CIEPs) in

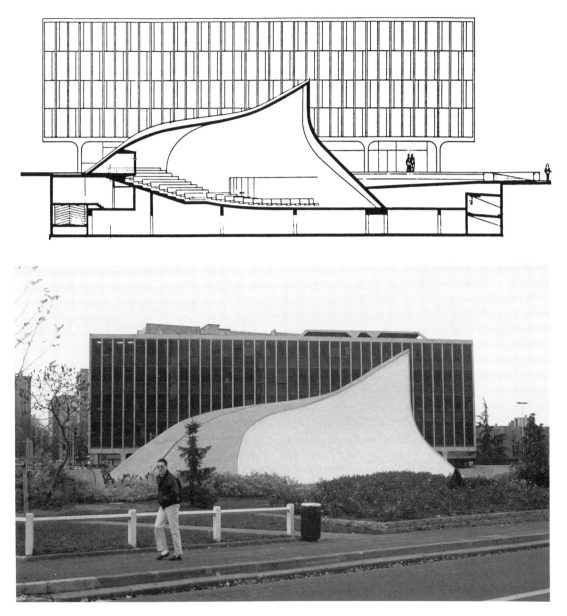

Figures 73–74. Niemeyer, Bourse de Travail, Bobigny, 1972–80. Formal contrasts of color, shape, and material enliven a Paris suburb of drab concrete slabs.

Figure 75. Niemeyer, Maison de la Culture, Le Havre, 1972–82. Niemeyer's dynamic forms seem warped by the blustery winds off the English Channel.

Figure 76. Maison de la Culture, Le Havre, plan. The center houses a state-of-the-art theater and a free-form, or poly-valent, exhibition space.

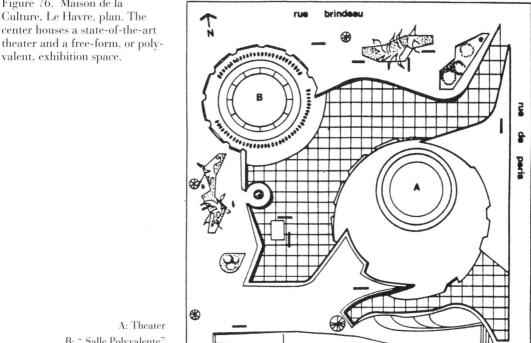

A: Theater
B: " Salle Polyvalente"

Figures 77–78. Maison de la Culture, Le Havre. The centerpiece of the design is the sunken pedestrian plaza, where the forms swirl as dramatically as the wind.

the state of Rio de Janeiro (begun 1984; fig. 79),
Niemeyer and his populist patrons, Governor
Leonel Brizola and his Secretary of Culture, Darcy
Ribeiro, sought to address one of Brazil's most
pressing problems: the crisis in primary education
in the public sector. Brizola proposed that five hun-
dred new public schools be erected in the state
where, at the start of 1983, 700,000 of its school-
age children were not served by the existing school
system and 52 percent of all students never finished
second grade.

To enact his "educational revolution," Brizola
commissioned Niemeyer, whose architectural solution called for a standardized school design that
could be repeated throughout the state and serve as
a nationwide model for educational reform.
Niemeyer proposed to accommodate a thousand
full-time students in centers containing twenty
classrooms, a library, medical and sports facilities,
and a cafeteria. Niemeyer's project used precast
modular elements of reinforced concrete to lower
costs and maximize construction efficiency. By the
end of 1987, 127 CIEPs had been constructed, 112

Figure 79. Niemeyer, Centro
Integrado de Educação Pública,
Rio de Janeiro, begun 1984. The
architect sought a low-cost, standardized solution for Rio's public
school crisis.

of which were functioning. But the highly polemical project was criticized for a number of faults, ranging from leaky roofs to high construction costs and poor acoustics. Press critics of Brizola and Ribeiro saw in the scheme an effort to consolidate electoral support among the state's poorest voters.

A related project involving Brizola, Ribeiro, and Niemeyer was Rio's Samba Stadium, popularly known as the Passarela do Samba or Sambódromo (1983–84). The project originated in the governor's perception that the public treasury was losing $7.5 million a year in subsidies to Rio's samba schools and in the construction of the temporary bleachers erected every year for the spectators of the carnival parade. Niemeyer was commissioned to come up with a "permanent architectural solution" for the performance and public observance of the spectacle. A permanent facility, Brizola believed, would eventually turn a profit for the city and help institutionalize carnival as a national symbol of Brazilian popular culture. At the head of the parade avenue, Niemeyer designed a huge (eighty-two-foot-tall) double-parabolic arch of reinforced concrete (fig. 80). This thin and elegant arch supports a concrete slab dramatically cantilevered out over a stepped stage area to form the focal point of Apotheosis Plaza, behind which a samba museum was installed. For the spectators along the parade avenue, Niemeyer and his structural engineer, José Carlos Sussekind, designed a series of monumental, cantilevered grandstands using modular elements of precast reinforced concrete. These massive structures, providing box seating above and general-admission standing room below, were intended to improve the spectators' visibility and sense of participation in the parade. Inside the grandstands, two hundred cubical rooms function as administrative offices during carnival and classrooms the rest of the year. When not in use as a stadium for carnival, the complex accommodates sixteen thousand

Figure 80. Niemeyer, Passarela do Samba (Sambódromo, or Samba Stadium), Rio de Janeiro, 1983–84. A new ritual center for the performance of the annual carnival spectacle, the complex functions the rest of the year as a public school.

students in what is touted as the largest school ever built in Brazil.

The Samba Stadium demonstrates Niemeyer's utopian conflation of educational reform, national ritual, and popular acculturation. His late masterpiece, the Memorial da América Latina in São Paulo (1989), is best understood as an expression of the persistence of this utopian impulse in modern Brazilian architecture. In the memorial Niemeyer again used precast concrete elements, but this time in the much more expressive, curvilinear shapes anticipated by the great arch of the Samba Stadium and his earlier free-form experiments. The memorial illustrates his effort to remake Latin American culture through a dynamic sculptural aesthetic that is as free in its form as it is unified in its conception and composition.

A monumental collaborative venture sponsored by the government of the state of São Paulo, the memorial (figs. 81–82) illustrates Niemeyer's effort to give harmonious abstract form to a project that was motivated by several conflicting visions of a better society for Brazil and Latin America. For Niemeyer and his patron, São Paulo Governor Orestes Qúercia, the official purpose of the memorial is to give concrete expression to the idea of Latin American integration and thus begin to realize that ambitious social project. The ensemble, divided by a multilane avenue, consists of two amorphous concrete compounds connected by a dramatically suspended, curving ramp-bridge for pedestrians. The complex has five major functional units housed in separate pavilions that recall exposition architecture: a ceremonial hall (Salão de Atos) for official gatherings and a collection of commemorative art (figs. 83 and 84); a library, the first in South America devoted exclusively to Latin American cultures (fig. 85); the Creativity Pavilion, containing permanent exhibits focusing on the craft production of the indigenous cultures of Latin America

Figure 81. Niemeyer, Memorial da América Latina, São Paulo, 1989, general view of complex showing the Brazilian Center for Latin American Studies, the suspended pedestrian ramp, and the bleeding hand sculpture. The memorial reflects a synthesis of Niemeyer's achievements in a multimedia ensemble devoted to the idea of Latin American unity.

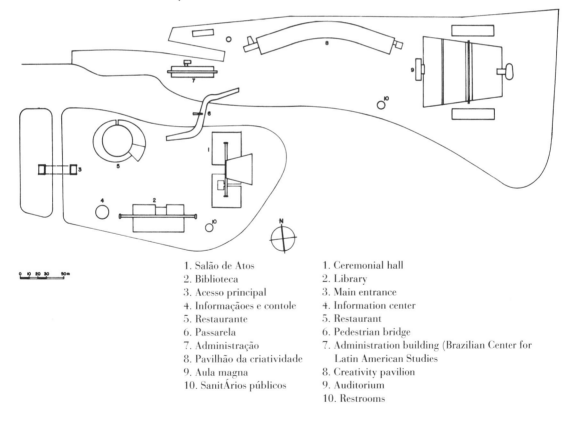

1. Salão de Atos
2. Biblioteca
3. Acesso principal
4. Informaçãoes e contole
5. Restaurante
6. Passarela
7. Administração
8. Pavilhão da criatividade
9. Aula magna
10. SanitÁrios públicos

1. Ceremonial hall
2. Library
3. Main entrance
4. Information center
5. Restaurant
6. Pedestrian bridge
7. Administration building (Brazilian Center for Latin American Studies
8. Creativity pavilion
9. Auditorium
10. Restrooms

Figure 82. Memorial da América Latina, plan of complex. The composition of the ensemble marks the high point of free-form complexity and Surrealistic biomorphism in Niemeyer's work.

Figure 83. Memorial da América Latina, Salão de Atos (ceremonial hall). The structures of the memorial, carried out under the guidance of the engineer José Sussekind, make use of huge prefab concrete elements painted white and finished with black-tinted plate glass. The Salão de Atos contains a number of important works by Brazilian artists such as Candido Portinari.

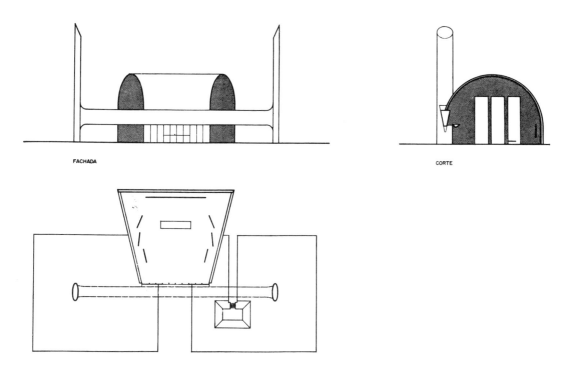

FACHADA

CORTE

Figure 84. Salão de Atos, elevation, section and plan. The curving vault springs from the beam supported by pylons on either side of the hall. The vaulted structure and pylons echo in abstracted form the sanctuary and bell towers of a great cathedral.

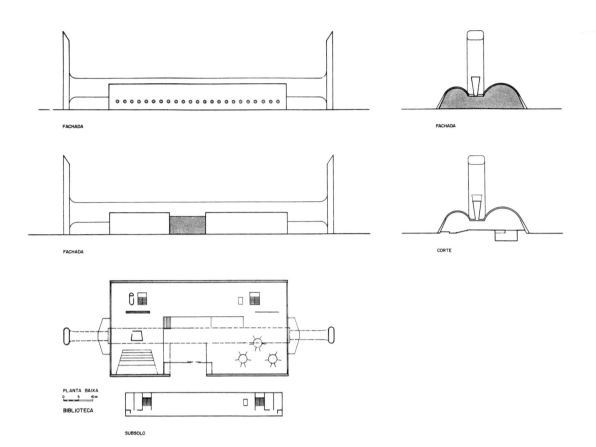

FACHADA

FACHADA

FACHADA

CORTE

PLANTA BAIXA
0   5   10 m
BIBLIOTECA

SUBSOLO

Figure 85. Memorial da América Latina, library, elevations, sections, and plan. The double vault of the library is suspended from the beam supported by the pylons. This allows the interior to be free of all structural support elements and maximizes ground space for shelving and reading rooms.

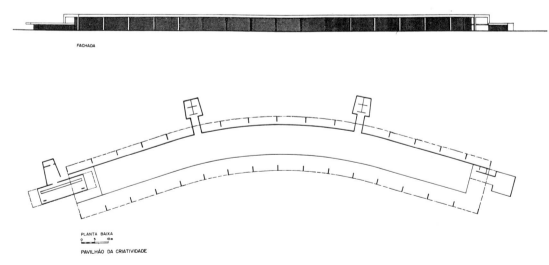

FACHADA

PLANTA BAIXA
0   5   10 m
PAVILHÃO DA CRIATIVIDADE

Figure 86. Memorial da América Latina, Pavilhão da Criatividade (Creativity Pavilion), elevation and plan. The pavilion houses a museum of the native arts and crafts of Latin America.

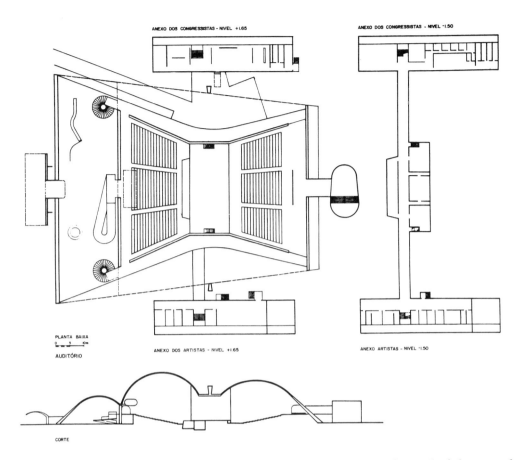

ANEXO DOS CONGRESSISTAS - NIVEL +1.65

ANEXO DOS CONGRESSISTAS - NIVEL -1.50

PLANTA BAIXA

0   5   10m

AUDITÓRIO

ANEXO DOS ARTISTAS - NIVEL +1.65

ANEXO ARTISTAS - NIVEL -1.50

CORTE

Figure 87. Memorial da América Latina, Aula Magna (auditorium), plan and elevation. The triple-vault structure is similar to that of the library.

(fig. 86); and, at the far end of the complex, the Aula Magna, a two-thousand-seat auditorium for congresses, musical and theatrical presentations, and other cultural events (fig. 87). The Brazilian Center for Latin American Studies, the heart of the memorial and its communication center, promotes the study of Latin American culture through scholarships, exchange programs, and monthly seminars (figs. 88 and 89).

The memorial's program of cultural unity derives from the thinking of the Brazilian social scientist and populist politician Darcy Ribeiro, who laments Latin America's political fragmentation and especially Brazil's historical isolation from its South American neighbors. Building the complex in São Paulo, Brazil's

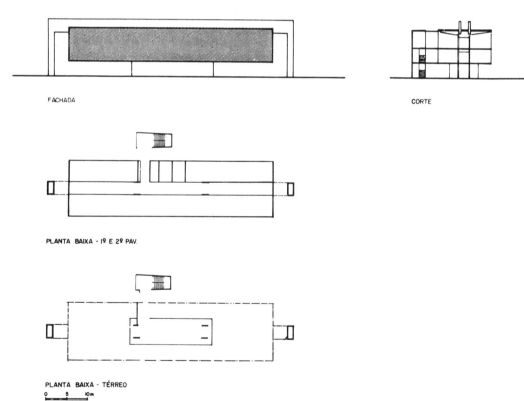

FACHADA

CORTE

PLANTA BAIXA - 1º E 2º PAV.

PLANTA BAIXA - TÉRREO

0   5   10m

ADMINISTRAÇÃO

Figures 88–89. Memorial da América Latina, Brazilian Center for Latin American Studies, main façade; elevation, section, and plans. The dramatically suspended structure of the center recalls that of the Museum of the City of Brasília and the São Paulo Art Museum (MASP) by Lino Bo Bardi.

largest and wealthiest city, was thus intended in part as a gesture to the rest of Latin America, signifying São Paulo's and thus Brazil's desire both to lead the project and participate in the community. The memorial provides a spatio-cultural forum, a central meeting place for all Latin American peoples, and a means to raise Brazilian and especially Paulista consciousness about Spanish and indigenous American cultures and what it means to be Latin American.

The seriousness of this ambitious project of cultural consciousness raising is reflected in the architectural forms of the library and the ceremonial hall. Both structures are framed by tall twin pillars, abstract and monumental, rising up majestically like the bell towers of a great Baroque church. In addition to providing a visual link with the verticality of the skyscrapers in the São Paulo cityscape beyond, thereby integrating the ensemble's horizontally spreading forms with their larger urban context, these towers function structurally—to anchor and support the horizontal beams upon which the roofs rest—and symbolically—to create a sense of ritual gravity and religious solemnity. Open to the public daily, the hall was intended to be "the most solemn space in São Paulo as well as the most popular."[47] It showcases several important works by Brazilian artists who seek to foster a reverence for the culture, history, and heroes of Latin America. Children are meant to feel inspired by Candido Portinari's mural depicting the martyrdom of Tiradentes, the hero of the thwarted movement for Brazil's national liberation, and by the bas-relief panels by Hector Paride Barnabó (a.k.a. Carybé) and Napoleon Potyguara Lazzaroto (Poty), which depict the ethnic diversity of Latin America's native and immigrant peoples. Spiritually moved to a heightened sense of cultural awareness by such images, the public may pursue in the library the deeper meanings of these artistic objects that convey lessons about Latin American history. The library and ceremonial hall are thus presented as modern cathedrals of Latin American culture and learning that seek to stimulate a new popular ritual—the contemplation and analysis of Latin diversity, liberation, and suffering—and to celebrate a new mass to a Latin America unified by these shared experiences.

Ribeiro and Niemeyer see the integration of all the arts into a unified multimedia ensemble as a metaphor for the integration of Latin American cultures. Perhaps the clearest visual expression of the memorial's theme is Bruno Giorgi's abstract marble sculpture *Integração* (*Integration*), which is composed of two inverted forms interlocking to create one (fig. 90). Live concerts by Latin American

Figure 90. Bruno Giorgi, *Integração* (in front of the Salão de Atos). Giorgi's abstract sculpture symbolizes the integration of opposites that is the major theme of the memorial.

musicians and a restaurant specializing in the region's varied cuisines add to the total immersion of the senses in Latin American culture.

Beneath the official agenda of integration, however, are several others. The memorial is one in a long tradition of great works sponsored by ambitious politicians seeking to leave their mark on history by bequeathing to society a monument of great import and popular appeal. Thus, the creation of the memorial emerged as a typically Brazilian ritual of political, economic, intellectual, and artistic collaboration in which a small group of powerful men pooled their resources in an attempt to change history with a landmark architectural development carried out in record time, in this case seventeen months. The memorial is thus being compared to Niemeyer's most successful monumental collaborations of the past. As Ribeiro notes, "By creating the Memorial, Governor Orestes Quércia repeats [ex-President] Juscelino Kubitschek's historic position that revolutionized Brazilian architecture in the 1940s, when he chose Oscar to build Pampulha." More importantly, he says, the memorial "will represent an architectural compound equivalent in its magnitude only to Brasília."[48] Quércia, who aspires to Brazil's presidency, claims to have dreamed of the memorial as a gubernatorial candidate, just as Kubitschek during his presidential campaign appealed to the popular idea of constructing a new capital for Brazil. For his part, Ribeiro situates the "Memorial Oscárico" alongside his own, more recent collaborative projects with Niemeyer: the Samba Stadium and the new public school system for Rio de Janeiro. These too were projects that sought to promote national culture and effect far-reaching reforms in Brazilian society.

Capitalist development interests in São Paulo were also an important impetus for the memorial project. Brazil's industrial elite, especially several major construction and engineering firms, materials suppliers, and manufacturers of decorative design products, see in the project an opportunity to market their enterprises throughout the continent. The São Paulo Metropolitan Subway Corporation, which provided major funding for the undertaking, sees the project not so much in terms of Latin American fraternity, but as a means to expand São Paulo's transportation infrastructure and stimulate public use of mass transit. The site selected for the memorial is adjacent to the new futuristic Barra Funda subway station, which the company would like to see emerge as a main transport and commercial hub for central São Paulo. Meanwhile, the minister of Housing and Urban Development sees the project as a convenient means to revitalize a rundown industrial district that was on the verge of being overtaken by shanties. A new shopping mall is planned.

Added to these special interests are Ribeiro and Niemeyer's desire to make the memorial express the ideals of Latin American unity and the Marxist dream of social justice. The project highlights the contradiction between Brazilian nationalist goals, the ambitions and capitalist interests of wealthy São Paulo, and the dream of Latin American integration. Ribeiro himself expresses a certain ambivalence in this respect: "This magnificent Oscaric ensemble, coupled with the ambitious cultural program, will make São Paulo into one of the cultural capitals of Latin America, giving Brazilians a nucleus around which to intensify solidarity amongst our people and cultivate a critical conscience of our reality and potential." Here he seems to be referring to Brazilian and especially Paulista realities and potentials, but he catches himself and quickly adds, "The Brazilian Center for Latin American Studies, the motor of the Memorial, faithful to the ideals of Bolívar, has, nevertheless, the fundamental objective of contributing to the creation of a Latin American nation, with a regional common market and a Latin American Parliament."[49] Although a building to house this parliament has recently been erected on the site of the memorial, it remains to be seen how the conflicting forces of nationalism, capitalism, continental integration, and social justice for the masses will be resolved.

Finally, there is Niemeyer's own aesthetic project—the obstinate search for a utopia of beauty—and his desire to transcend politics (almost) entirely by creating an inspiring work of beautiful art that will, through its great unity and monumentality, lift the humanity that beholds it, if only momentarily, out of the dismal grind of urban existence in modern-day São Paulo. Niemeyer's ensemble attempts to resolve artistically the conflicts and contradictions of the integration project through an uncompromising abstraction within which freedom and unity, the twin pillars of this utopia, coexist harmoniously on the aesthetic level. The free-form layout and the formal diversity of the pavilions, unified by the opposition of flat black glass and curving white concrete common to all, illustrate this effort.

In designing the complex, Niemeyer sought to create a monumental "architectural spectacle" that would reflect the serious theme of the memorial (fig. 91). The complex is to be experienced by commuters who, emerging from the depths of the adjacent subway station, will "be inspired by the enormous impact of this architectural wonder." Niemeyer describes his intentions in these terms: "While designing the Memorial, my greatest concern was to make it so different, so free and creative, imbued with such plastic unity that it would incite, right from the start, the astonishment every work of art must inspire."[50] He sought to create an element of surprise and marvel through daring structural acrobatics, exemplified by his "free-in-

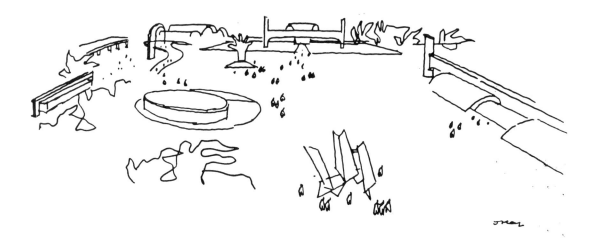

the-air" pedestrian bridge and the suspended design of the Center for Latin American Studies (fig.
88), which recalls his museum in Brasília (fig. 53)
and the São Paulo Art Museum by Lina Bo Bardi.

Such apparently magical structures and the per-
petuation of the myth of the genius are of course
typical of Niemeyer and the modernist utopian project. Echoing Lúcio Costa's method in designing the
winning plan for Brasília, he describes how his inspired perspective for the memorial complex came
to him spontaneously "as if a premonition had suddenly taken hold."[51] Be that as it may, the progres-
sion of spaces and one's visual experience of the
buildings and sculptural objects in this Corbusian
architectural promenade appear to have been care-
fully thought out by Niemeyer. Sensitive to basic
human instincts like hunger, thirst, and spending
money, he placed the restaurant directly adjacent
to the stairway by which weary subway commuters
enter the complex. This delicious solution of course
increases the likelihood that this potentially lucra-
tive aspect of the memorial's "cultural program"
will be well patronized.

Once out of the snack bar, however, it is practi-
cally impossible to approach the Salão de Atos, the
ritual focus of the complex, without first passing by

and coming to terms with what Niemeyer intended to be the sculptural centerpiece of the complex. His dramatic "gesture of human solidarity" is a huge, twenty-three-foot-tall open hand in reinforced concrete (fig. 92), one that recalls Le Corbusier's *Monument to the Open Hand* at Chandigarh. More than a tribute to Le Corbusier—an appropriate summation of the Brazilian's fundamental artistic debt to the Franco-Swiss master—Niemeyer's open hand also expresses the frustrations of a continent exploited by Western imperialism. For here is depicted what Eduardo Galeano calls the "open veins of Latin America,"[52] a hand spread out with desperate splayed fingers, a stigmata with a map of Latin America trickling sacrificial "blood" down its wrist. The original inscription Niemeyer intended was to have read: "Sweat, blood, and poverty have marked the history of this oppressed Latin America. Now we must unite it, defend it, and make it independent and content." At Governor Quércia's insistence, Niemeyer toned down his political invective. Later the architect wrote: "This is a hand that reminds us of past days of strife, poverty, and abandonment." But mindful that that past is still part of the present for many, he added: "Life is full of sorrow and happiness—'twin sisters'—as Jorge Luis Borges called them, but we must never forget that, long before him, old Marx said we ourselves must change it."[53] If socioeconomic integration is the dream for the future of Latin America, Niemeyer's bleeding hand reminds us of the serious inequalities of the past and present that must be overcome to make that dream come true. But it also calls into question the viability of a capitalist model for integration. A Marxist call to arms in a monument patronized by state capitalism and wealthy Paulistas? This is typical of Oscar Niemeyer.

So is the dialogue he maintains with his "double" on the conflict between social responsibility and

Figure 92. Niemeyer, Memorial da América Latina, drawing of bleeding hand sculpture. A Marxist protest as the centerpiece of a complex erected by state capitalism and wealthy Paulistas? This is typically Oscaric!

monumental architecture. Fully aware that the memorial represents a model of social integration molded by the Brazilian elite of which he is an ambivalent part, he explains apologetically:

I have done very few projects of a social nature, and I must admit that whenever I do one, I feel like I'm conniving with the demagogic and paternalistic objective they stand for, fooling the working class that demands higher wages and the advantage of having better opportunities. . . . On the other hand, I never felt afraid of monumentality when the theme in itself demanded it. After all, what remained of architecture over the ages were the monumental works, those that represent the evolution of techniques—those which, fair or unfair from the social point of view, still manage to move us. Beauty imposes itself on the sensibility of men.[54]

As he concluded long ago, when designing Brasília, "It is strange how the power of beauty makes us forget so much injustice."[55]

The function of Niemeyer's art, then, is to create an aesthetic utopia that visually nourishes the Latin American spirit and thus enables it to put up with the harsh day-to-day reality that the architect cannot change. But at the same time, he shuns art as social escapism by inserting into his utopian ensembles politically charged elements like the bleeding hand—brutal elements that shock through contrast and thereby remind us of the flip side of the beauty: the injustice, the lost communist alternative, the anger Niemeyer and many Latin Americans feel about the failed utopia that was supposed to bring more just social development to the people.

The memorial is thus a study in contrasting but inseparable twins: black and white; ugly industrial city and pretty utopian ensemble; the monumental and the socially responsible; forgetfulness and the remembrance of things past (and present); the abstract and the general over the detailed and the specific; sorrow and happiness; rich and poor; Marxist rhetoric and capitalist reality; Brazilian and Latin American. What unifies these twins is their status as twins. What brings unity to the free forms of Niemeyer's pavilions and to the diversity of Latin American peoples is the shared experience, or at least the perception, of extreme contrasts. Niemeyer's abstract resolution, really his white-washing of this dialectic itinerary, is what lends his work to such a wide variety of different causes, in-terests, and multiple meanings. The vague visual rhetoric of abstract formalism is the key: no room for details here, just pure and sensual form, he emphasizes.

Niemeyer continues to be criticized for a lack of sensitivity to the details of human use. The memorial has been attacked as a cold and unwel-coming place, as yet another example of concrete monotony that could have been relieved by a tropi-cal garden by the Brazilian landscape designer Roberto Burle Marx. There are few places to sit and no shade except that provided by the long shadows of the buildings. Nor have the palm trees that were recently planted on the site done much to change this situation. On a typical summer's day, the heat and near blinding light of the tropical sun reflected off the burning concrete force one to seek refuge in one of the pavilions, where the environment is at least cooler if not more inviting. Despite the open-ness of the space, the compound can have the closed feeling of a military precinct: tall fences and security gates make it difficult for the man off the street to get in. Like Niemeyer's Samba Stadium, it comes alive only when it is filled with people.

Yet for all its social shortcomings, the memorial illustrates not only the refinement of Niemeyer's structural and compositional techniques, but also the maturation of his late style into a Surrealistically expressive art that reflects the persistence of his unique approach to architecture—an approach characterized by the effort to resolve (or wish away) the contradictions of existing realities in a harmonious visual synthesis that, like an expensive carnival costume, elegantly masks the unresolved conflicts underneath. As in carnival, the basis of the unity and the ritual is the inversion itself.

At age eighty-six, Oscar Niemeyer has become an enduring Latin American tradition, one perhaps entitled to one last great ritual of utopian modernism, with all its inherent contradictions. But Niemeyer himself does not yet seem to realize that his innovations now seem quite old, not nearly as shocking as they were thirty years ago. The scale, budget, and power of the utopian project have been drastically reduced, but the rhetoric and ambitions have, if anything, expanded. Whereas the builders of Brasília asked only for the faith of the Brazilians, the builders of this much less grandiose memorial are asking all of Latin America to buy this conflict-laden vision of utopia. One wonders whether that utopia will ever get more concrete than it does here.

In the final analysis, what is most important for Niemeyer is good form and, more specifically, the sweeping arc and the flowing curve. This book has argued that understanding the source of his infatuation with the curvilinear biomorphic forms that characterize works such as the memorial leads us to a deeper appreciation of the artist. Niemeyer's design studio in Rio de Janeiro features a spectacular view of Copacabana Beach and Sugar Loaf Mountain. So Le Corbusier was quite right when he aptly observed that Niemeyer has the mountains of Rio in his eyes. But, as this book has suggested, Niemeyer sees more: "It is not the right angle that attracts me, nor the straight line, hard and inflexible, created by man. What attracts me is the free and sensual curve—the curve that I find in the mountains of my country, in the sinuous course of its rivers, in the body of the beloved woman. The entire universe is made of curves—the curved universe of Einstein."[56]

"But, Mr. Niemeyer," asks the art historian, "which of these is in the end the most important? Einstein? The mountains?"

The architect pauses, looks down upon his own special Brazilian universe—upon the contour of the crescent beach and the human architecture stretched out upon the sand—and answers: "Woman. Woman is the most important of all."[57]

NOTES

1. Oscar Niemeyer, *Oscar Niemeyer* (Lausanne: Alphabet, 1977), 11.

2. Ibid., 12.

3. Ibid., 13.

4. For a collection of primary texts dealing with the contributions of Costa, Niemeyer, and others, see Alberto Xavier et al., *Arquitetura Moderna Brasileira: Depoimento de uma geração* (São Paulo: Pini, Associação Brasileira de Ensino de Arquitetura e Fundação Vilanova Artigas, 1987).

5. Leopoldo Castedo, *The Baroque Prevalence in Brazilian Art* (New York: Charles Frank, 1964).

6. Niemeyer, *Oscar Niemeyer*, 217.

7. For a good discussion of Le Corbusier's activity in Brazil, see Elizabeth Harris, *Le Corbusier: Riscos Brasileiros* (São Paulo: Nobel, 1987).

8. Le Corbusier, *Precisions on the Present State of Architecture and City Planning*, tr. Edith Schreiber Aujame (Cambridge and London: MIT Press, 1991), 7.

9. Ibid., 5.

10. Ibid., 142–43.

11. Ibid., 143.

12. Quoted in Geraldo Mayrink, "Toque de Nobreza," *Veja* (January 1993): 74.

13. Le Corbusier, *Precisions*, 15.

14. Quoted in Xavier, *Arquitetura Moderna Brasileira*, 94.

15. Le Corbusier, *Precisions*, 30–32.

16. Ibid., 245.

17. Le Corbusier, *Towards a New Architecture*, tr. Frederick Etchells (New York: Dover, 1986), 215, 153.

18. Le Corbusier, *Precisions*, 1–2.

19. Ibid., 233, 235.

20. Ibid., 29.

21. Ibid., 9.

22. Ibid., 26.

23. Oscar Niemeyer, "Depoimento de 24 de maio," in *A sedução* (Rio de Janeiro: Terceira Margem, 1989), 23.

24. Le Corbusier, *Precisions*, 236.

25. Oscar Niemeyer, *Meu sósia e eu* (Rio de Janeiro: Revan, 1992), 125.

26. Ibid.

27. Consider, for instance, the comments of the Swiss

functionalist Max Bill, who wrote of Niemeyer's experiments with pilotis:

"In a street here in São Paulo I have seen under construction a building in which *pilotis* construction is carried to extremes one would have supposed impossible. There I saw some shocking things, modern architecture sunk to the depths, a riot of anti-social waste, lacking any sense of responsibility toward either the business occupant or his customers. . . . Thick *pilotis*, thin *pilotis*, *pilotis* of whimsical shapes lacking any structural rhyme or reason, disposed all over the place. . . . One is baffled to account for such barbarism as this in a country where there is a CIAM group, a country in which international congresses are held, where a journal like *Habitat* is published and where there is a biennial exhibition of architecture. For such works are born of a spirit devoid of all decency and of all responsibility to human needs. It is the spirit of decorativeness, something diametrically opposed to the spirit which animates architecture, which is the art of building, the social art above all others." Quoted in Kenneth Frampton, *Modern Architecture: A Critical History* (New York: Thames and Hudson, 1985), 257.

28. Le Corbusier, *Towards a New Architecture*, 191.

29. Quoted in Sarane Alexandrian, *Surrealist Art* (New York: Thames and Hudson, 1985), 7.

30. Le Corbusier, *Towards a New Architecture*, 191.

31. Niemeyer, *Meu sósia e eu.*

32. Ibid., 11.

33. Ibid., 71.

34. Le Corbusier, *Towards a New Architecture*, 151.

35. Quoted in Alexandrian, *Surrealist Art*, 141.

36. Ernesto Rogers, *Architectural Review* 116 (October 1954): 240.

37. Quoted in Alexandrian, *Surrealist Art*, 59.

38. Niemeyer, *Meu sósia e eu*, 76.

39. Le Corbusier, *Towards a New Architecture*, 73–74.

40. Alexandrian, *Surrealist Art*, 9.

41. Ibid., 49.

42. Ibid., 220.

43. Le Corbusier, *Towards a New Architecture*, 187.

44. Quoted in Norma Evenson, *Two Brazilian Capitals: Architecture and Urbanism in Rio de Janeiro and Brasília* (New Haven and London: Yale University Press, 1973), 204.

45. Niemeyer, "Nuvens," in *Meu sósia e eu*, 59. The Portuguese text reads: "Sempre que viajava de carro para Brasília, minha distração era olhar as nuvens do céu. Quantas coisas inesperadas elas surgerem! Às vezes são catedrais enormes e misteriosas, as catedrais de Exupéry com certeza; outras vezes, guerreiros terríveis, carros romanos a cavalgarem pelos ares; outros ainda, monstros desconhecidos a correrem pelos ventos em louca disparada e, mais frequentemente porque sempre as procurava, lindas e vaporosas mulheres recostadas nas nuvens, a sorrirem para mim dos espaços infinitos.

Mas logo tudo se transformava: as catedrais se desvaneciam em branco nevoeiro, os guerreiros viravam prestitos carnavalescos intermináveis; os monstros se escondiam em escuras cavernas, para surgirem adiante mais furiosos ainda, e as mulheres iam se esgarçando, se estendendo, transformadas em pássaros ou negras serpentes.

Muitos vezes pensei fotografar tudo isso, tão exatas eram as figuras que apareciam. Nunca o fiz.

Mas, sempre que viajo, olhar para as nuvens é a minha distração predileto, curioso, procurando decifrá-las como se estivesse em busca de uma boa e esperada mensagem. Naquele dia, porém, a visão foi mais surpreendente. Era uma bela mulher, rosada como uma figura de Renoir. O rosto oval, os seios fartos, a ventre liso, e as pernas longas a se entrelaçarem nas nuvens brancas do céu.

E fiquei a olhá-la embevecido, com medo de que se diluísse de repente. Mas os ventos daquela tarde de verão me deviam estar ouvindo e durante muito tempo ela ali ficou a me olhar de longe, como a convidar-me para subir, e com ela, entre as nuvens, brincar um pouco.

Mas o que temia tinha de acontecer. E pouco a pouco a minha namorada foi se diluindo, os braços se alongando com desespero, os seios a voaram como se destacando do corpo, as longas pernas se contorcendo em espiral,

como se dali ela não quisesse sair. Só os olhos continu-
avam a me fitar, cada vez maiores, cheios de espanto e
tristeza, quando uma nuvem maior, densa e negra, a lev-
ou para longe de mim.

E continuei a segui-la, inquieto, vendo a lutar entre as
nuvens que a envolviam, fustigada pela fúria dos ventos
que a dilaceravam impiedosamente.

E senti como aquela metamorfose perversa se
assemelhava ao nosso próprio destino, obrigados a
nascer, crescer, lutar, morrer e desaparecer para sempre,
como ocorria com aquela bela figura de mulher."

46. Le Corbusier, *Towards a New Architecture*, 203.

47. Darcy Ribeiro's comments are found in *Módulo* 100
(1989): 11–13.

48. Ibid.

49. Ibid., 13.

50. Ibid., 27, 37.

51. *Memorial da América Latina* (São Paulo: Fundação
Memorial da América Latina, 1989), 12.

52. Eduardo Galeano, *Open Veins of Latin America*
(New York: Monthly Review Press, 1973).

53. *Módulo* 100 (1989): 37.

54. Ibid, 23.

55. Oscar Niemeyer, "The Contemporary City," *Módulo*
11 (1958): 5.

56. This is my own translation of an oft-quoted passage
that Niemeyer sometimes uses to explain his architecture. See his essay "De Pampulha ao Memorial da
América Latina," *Módulo* 100 (1989): 15, and *Meu
sósia e eu*.

57. Personal communication with the author, Rio de
Janeiro, May 1990.

SELECTED BIBLIOGRAPHY

I. General Works on Brazilian Architecture

Bruand, Yves. *Arquitetura contemporânea no Brasil.* São Paulo: Perspectiva, 1981.

Evenson, Norma. *Two Brazilian Capitals: Architecture and Urbanism in Rio de Janeiro and Brasília.* New Haven and London: Yale University Press, 1973.

Fils, Alexander. *Brasília: Modern Architektur und Stadtplannung in Brasilien.* Dusseldorf: Beton, 1987.

Hitchcock, Henry Russell. *Latin American Architecture since 1945.* New York: Museum of Modern Art, 1955.

Holston, James. *The Modernist City: An Anthropological Critique of Brasília.* Chicago and London: University of Chicago Press, 1989.

Mindlin, Henrique. *Modern Architecture in Brazil.* New York: Reinhold, 1956.

II. Monographs on Niemeyer

Fils, Alexander. *Oscar Niemeyer.* Berlin: Frolich and Kaufmann, 1982.

Hornig, Christian. *Oscar Niemeyer: Bauten und Projekte.* Munich: Heinz Moos, 1981.

Luigi, Gilbert. *Oscar Niemeyer: une esthetique de la fluidité.* Marseilles: Parenthèses, 1987.

Papadaki, Stamo. *The Work of Oscar Niemeyer.* New York: Reinhold, 1954.

———. *Oscar Niemeyer: Works in Progress.* New York: Reinhold, 1956.

———. *Oscar Niemeyer.* New York: Braziller, 1960.

Puppi, Lionello. *A Arquitetura de Oscar Niemeyer.* Rio de Janeiro: Revan, 1988.

Spade, Rupert. *Oscar Niemeyer.* London: Thames and Hudson, 1971.

III. Articles by Niemeyer in *Módulo* (Rio de Janeiro)

"Problemas atuais da arquitetura brasileira." 3 (1955): 19–22.

"A Capela de Ronchamp." 5 (1956): 40–45.

"Niemeyer fala sobre Brasília." 6 (1956): 8–23.

"Consideraçoes sobre a arquitetura brasileira." 7 (1957): 5–10.

"Depoimento." 9 (1958): 3–6.

"A Catedral." 11 (1958): 7–15.

"A Imaginação na arquitetura." 15 (1959): 6–13.

"Forma e função na arquitetura." 21 (1960): 3–7.

"Joaquim Cardozo." 26 (1961): 4–7.

"Habitação pre-fabricada em Brasília." 27 (1962): 27–38.

"Consideraçoes sobre a arquitetura." 44 (1976): 34–40.

"Viagens. Origens e influências na arquitetura." 46 (1977): 31–34.

"Problemas da arquitetura 1: o espaço arquitetural." 50 (1978): 54–61.

"Problemas da arquitetura 2: as fachadas de vidro." 51 (1978): 44–47.

"Problemas da arquitetura 3: arquitetura e técnica estrutural." 52 (1978): 34–38.

"Problemas da arquitetura 4: o préfabricado e a arquitetura." 53 (1979): 56–59.

"Problemas da arquitetura 5: o mercado de trabalho." 54 (1979): 94–95.

"Problemas da arquitetura 6: o problema estrutural e a arquitetura contemporânea." 57 (1980): 94–97.

"Problemas da arquitetura 7: método de trabalho." 58 (1980): 86–89.

IV. Special Editions of *Módulo* Dealing with Niemeyer

Catálogo Oficial da Exposição Oscar Niemeyer, Congresso. "Cidades do Futuro," Sao Paulo, August 1985.

Brasília, 26 anos. 89–90 (1986).

Oscar Niemeyer, 50 anos de arquitetura. 97 (1988).

Memorial da América Latina. 100 (1989)

V. Books by Niemeyer

Minha experiencia em Brasília. Rio de Janeiro: Vitoria, 1961.

Quase memórias: viagens, tempos de entusiasmo e revolta, 1961–1966. Rio de Janeiro: Civilização Brasileira, 1968.

Oscar Niemeyer. Milan: Mondadori, 1975 (French edition, Lausanne: Alphabet, 1977).

A Forma em arquitetura. Rio de Janeiro: Avenir, 1978.

Rio: de provincia a metropole. Rio de Janeiro: Colorama, 1980.

Oscar Niemeyer. São Paulo: Almed, 1985.

Meu sósia e eu. Rio de Janeiro: Revan, 1992.